EASY PIANO

Gospel Songs of Devotion

T0045019

ISBN 978-0-634-02247-0

HAL•LEONARD®
CORPORATION
7777 W. BLUEMOUND RD. P.O. BOX 13819 MILWAUKEE, WI 53213

Visit Hal Leonard Online at
www.halleonard.com

AMAZING GRACE

Words by JOHN NEWTON
From *A Collection of Sacred Ballads*
Traditional American Melody
From Carrell and Clayton's *Virginia Harmony*
Arranged by EDWIN O. EXCELL

Slowly, with reverence

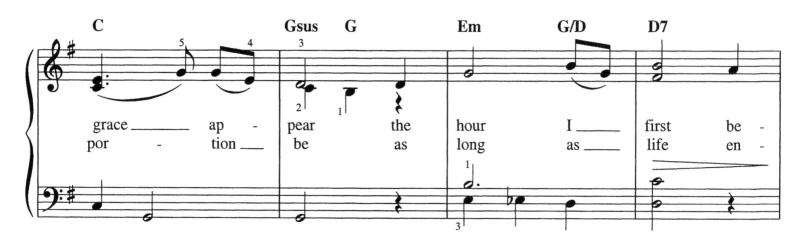

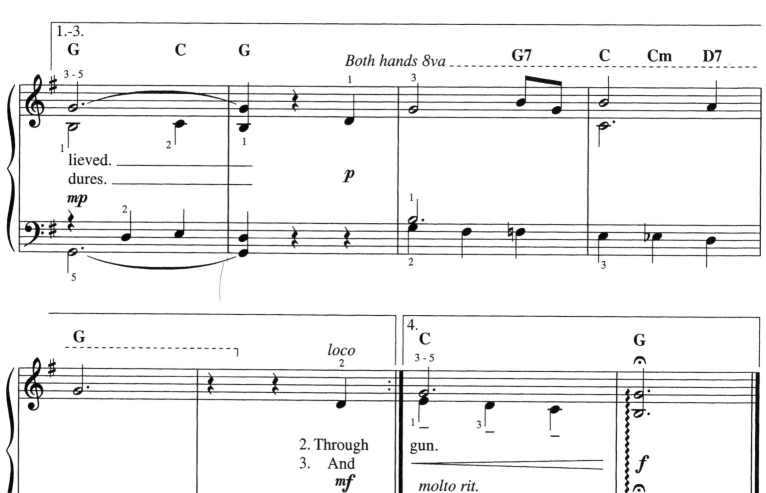

Additional Verses

3. And when this flesh and heart shall fail
   And mortal life shall cease,
   I shall possess within the veil
   A life of joy and peace.

4. When we've been there ten thousand years,
   Bright shining as the sun,
   We've no less days to sing God's praise
   Than when we first begun.

BECAUSE HE LIVES

Words by WILLIAM J. and GLORIA GAITHER
Music by WILLIAM J. GAITHER

Moderately

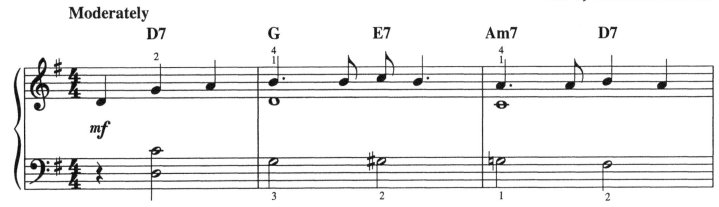

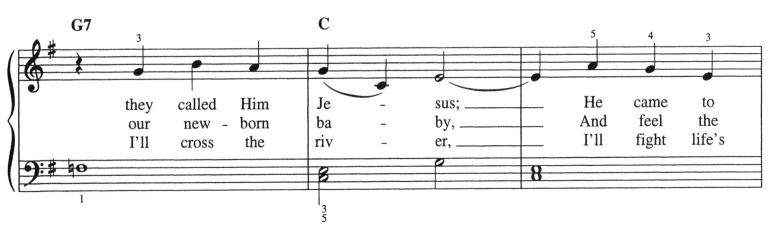

God sent His Son,
hold day

they called Him
our new-born
I'll cross the

Je — sus; ___
ba ___
riv — er, ___

He came to
And feel the
I'll fight life's

love, ___
pride ___
fi — ___

heal and for —
and joy he
nal war with

give. ___
gives. ___
pain. ___

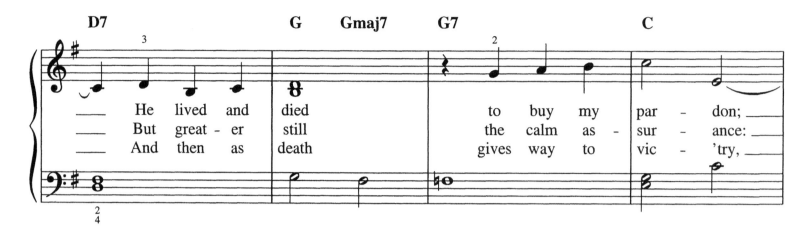

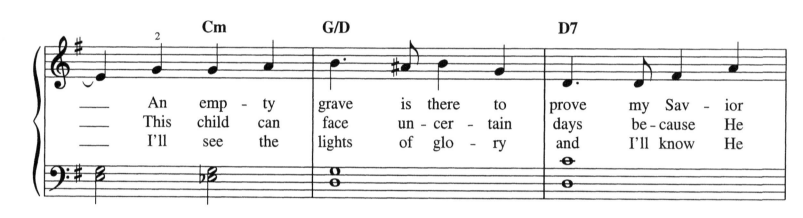

THE BLOOD WILL NEVER LOSE ITS POWER

Words and Music by
ANDRAÉ CROUCH

CLIMB EV'RY MOUNTAIN
from THE SOUND OF MUSIC

Lyrics by OSCAR HAMMERSTEIN II
Music by RICHARD RODGERS

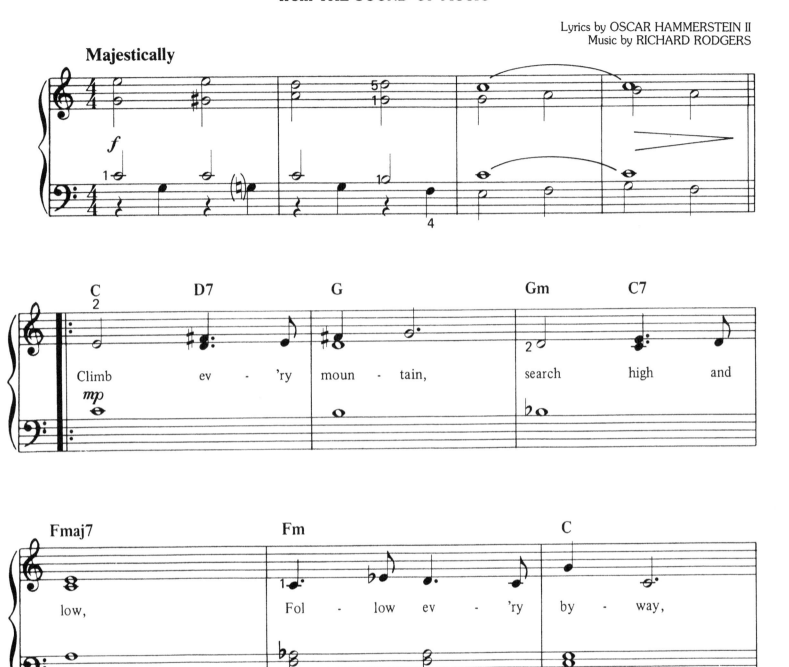

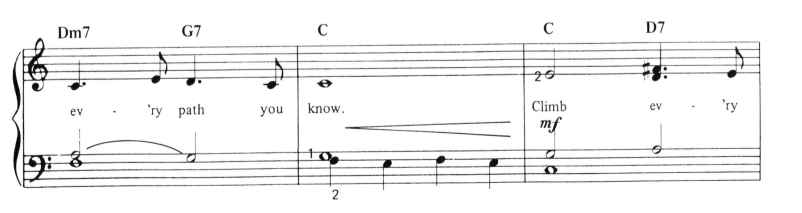

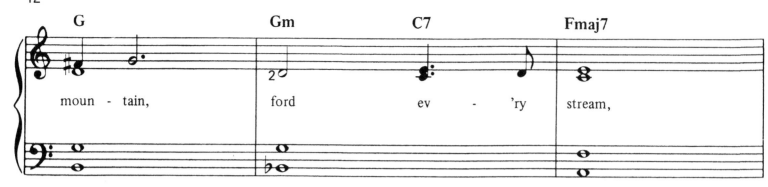

moun - tain, ford ev - 'ry stream,

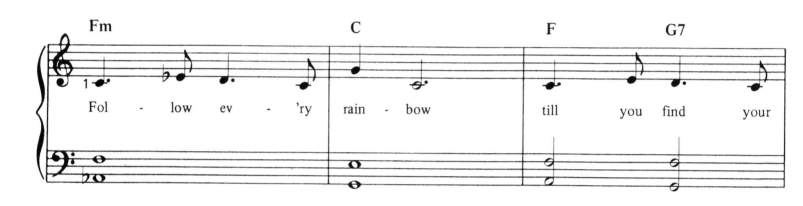

Fol - low ev - 'ry rain - bow till you find your

dream! A dream that will need all the love you can

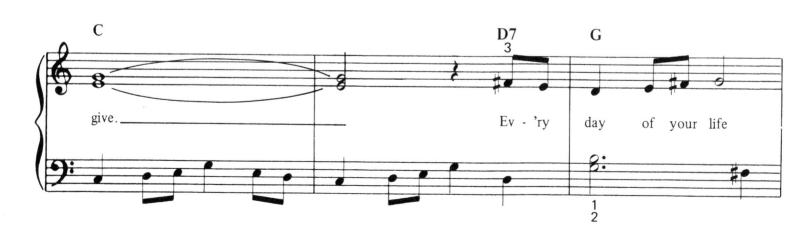

give. _____ Ev - 'ry day of your life

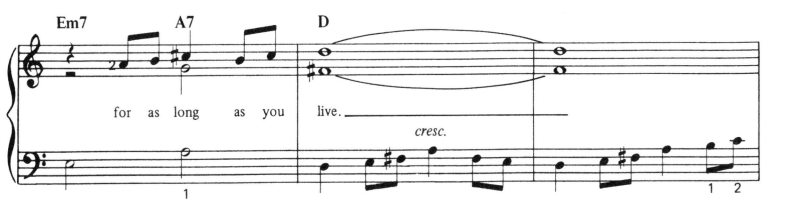

for as long as you live. _____

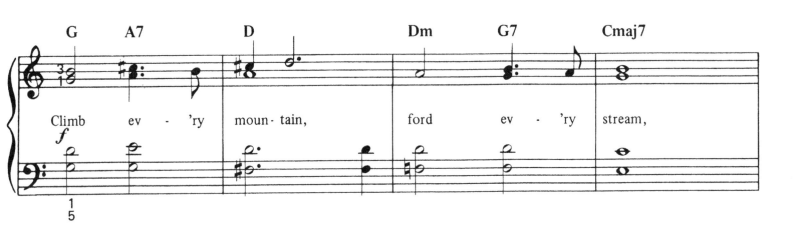

Climb ev- 'ry moun- tain, ford ev- 'ry stream,

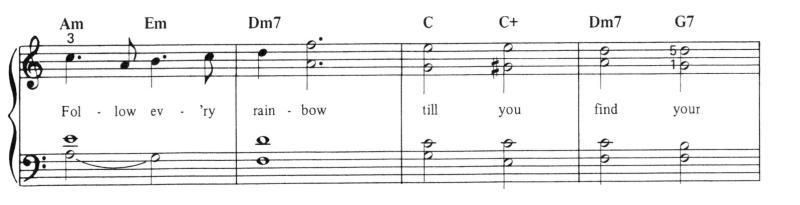

Fol - low ev- 'ry rain - bow till you find your

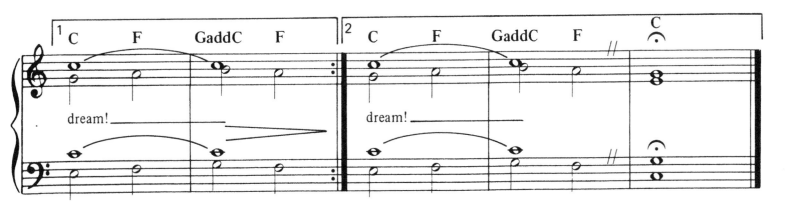

dream! _____ dream! _____

EL SHADDAI

Words and Music by MICHAEL CARD
and JOHN THOMPSON

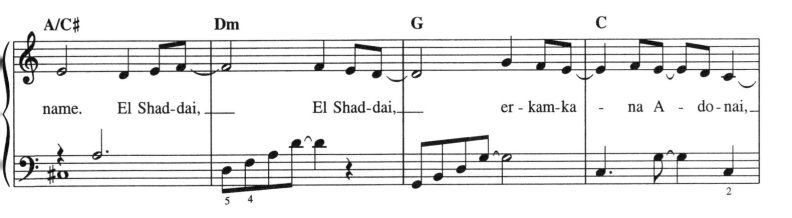

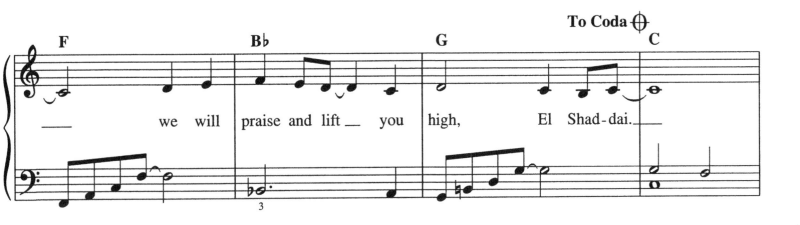

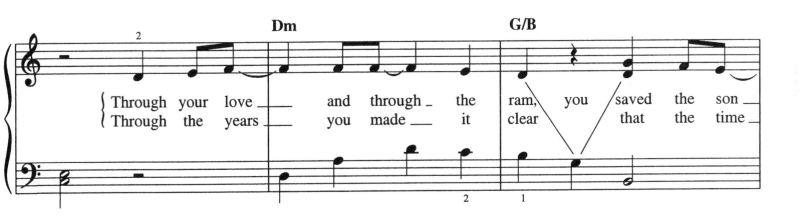

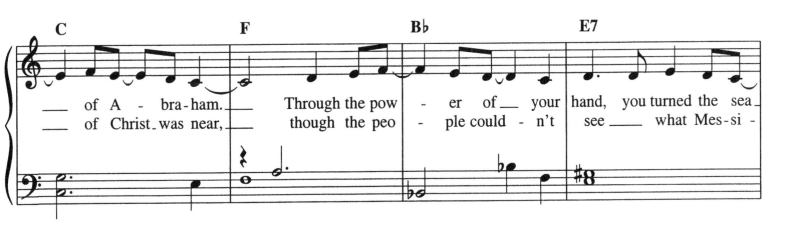

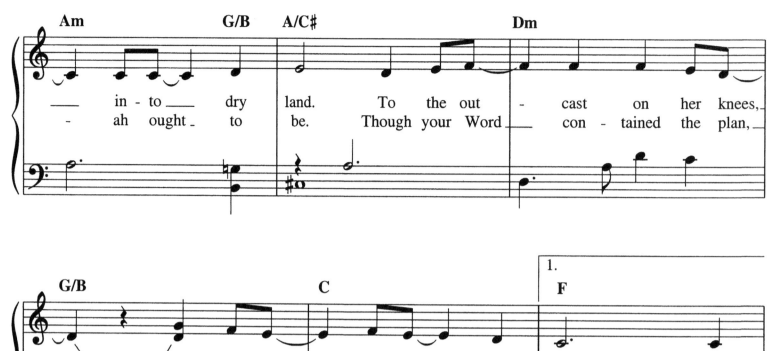

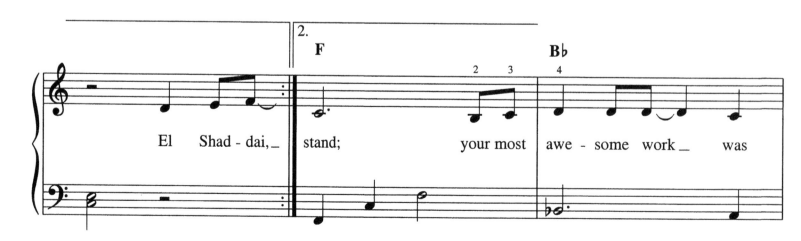

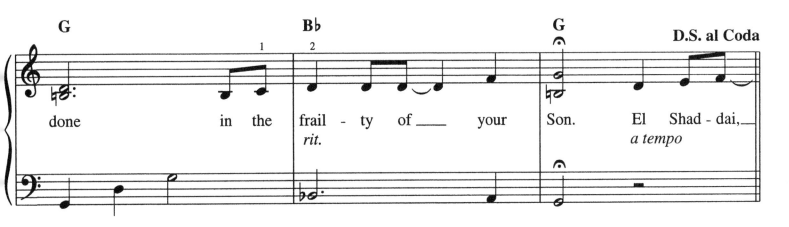

D.S. al Coda

done in the frail - ty of ____ your Son. El Shad - dai,

rit.   *a tempo*

CODA

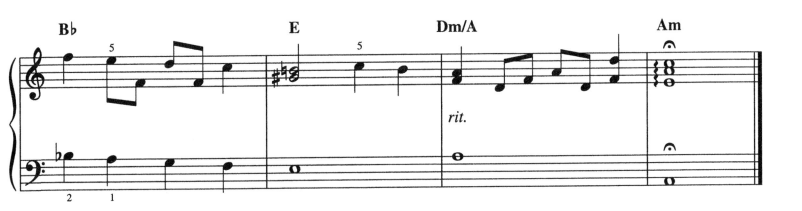

EVERYTHING IS BEAUTIFUL

Words and Music by
RAY STEVENS

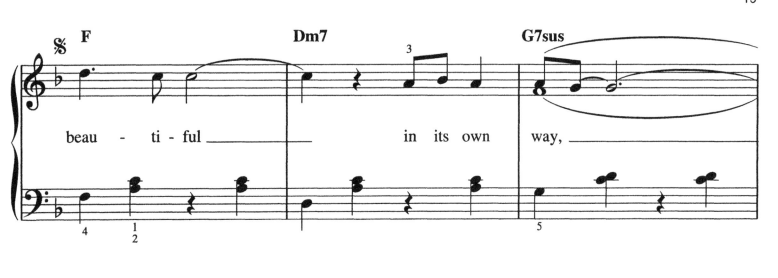

beau - ti - ful _____ in its own way, _____

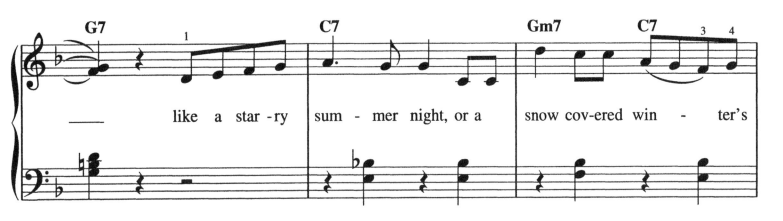

_____ like a star - ry sum - mer night, or a snow cov-ered win - ter's

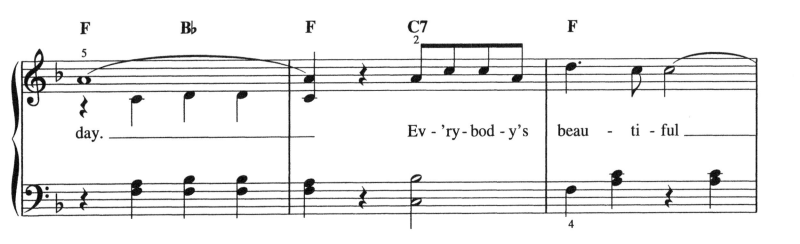

day. _____ Ev - 'ry - bod - y's beau - ti - ful _____

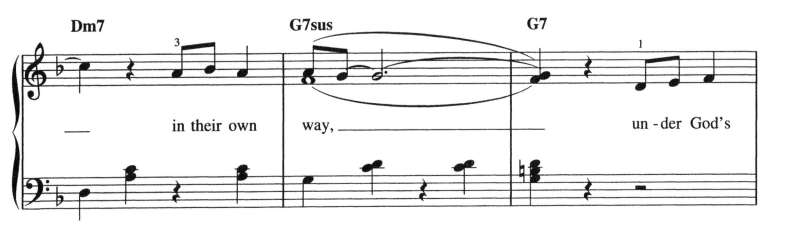

_____ in their own way, _____ un - der God's

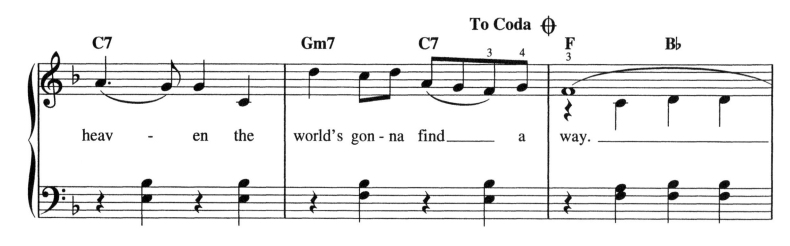

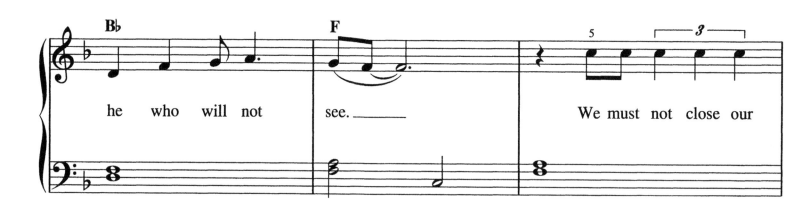

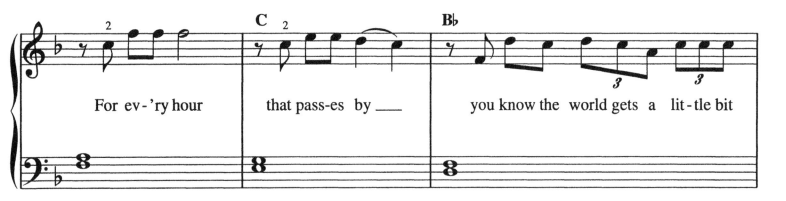

For ev-'ry hour | that pass-es by ___ | you know the world gets a lit-tle bit

old - er. | It's time to re-al-ize | that beau-ty lies in the

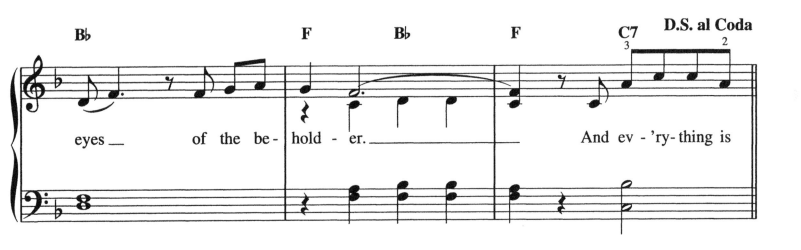

eyes ___ of the be-|hold - er.___ | And ev-'ry-thing is

CODA

way. ___

THE FAMILY OF GOD

Words by WILLIAM J. and GLORIA GAITHER
Music by WILLIAM J. GAITHER

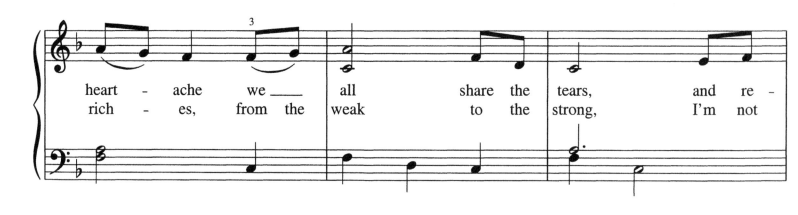

heart - ache we ___ all share the tears, and re -
rich - es, from the weak to the strong, I'm not

C7   **Gm7**   **C7**

joice in each vic - t'ry in this fam - 'ly so
wor - thy to be ___ here, but praise God I be -

1. **F**   **C7**   2. **F**   **Db7**

dear.   I'm so   long!

CODA

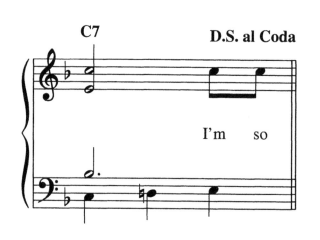

C7   **D.S. al Coda**

I'm so

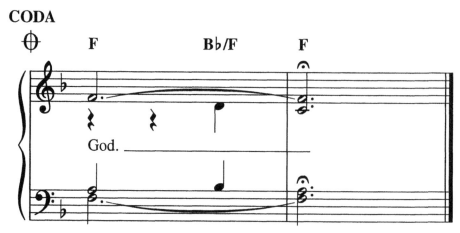

F   **Bb/F**   **F**

God. _____

HE GREW THE TREE

By CHUCK LAWRENCE

Reflectively

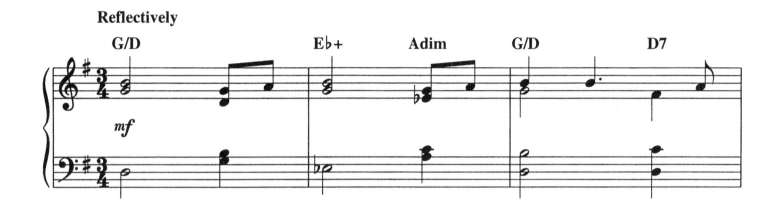

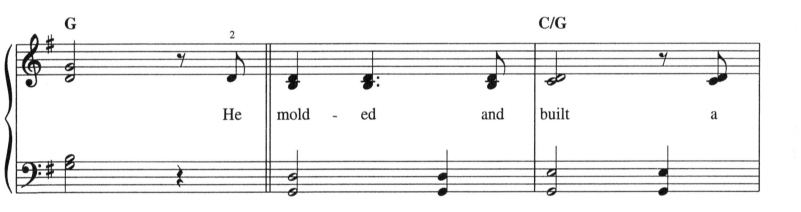

He mold - ed and built a

small lone - ly hill that He knew would be

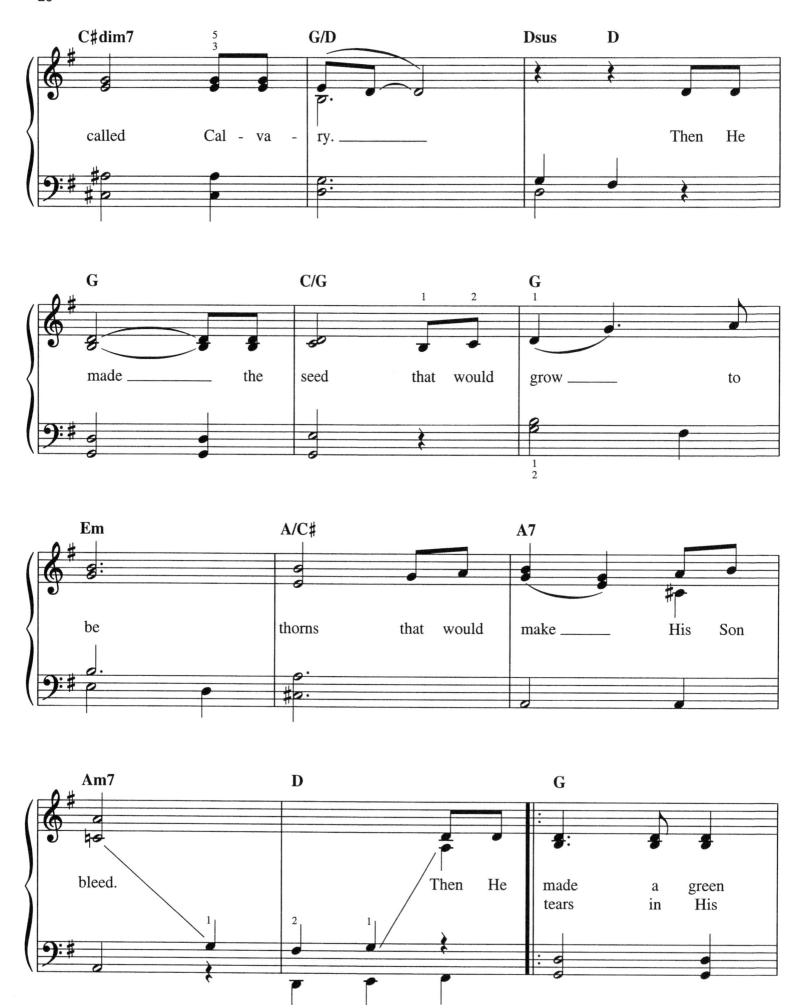

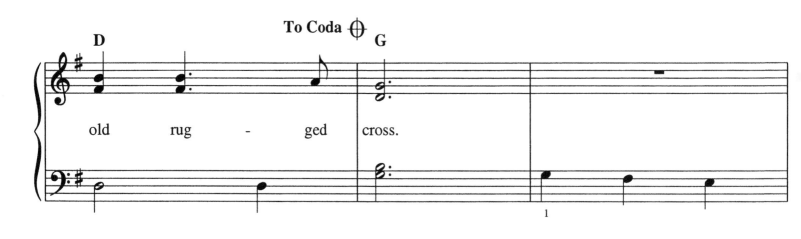

old rug - ged cross.

Noth - ing took His life; _____ with love He

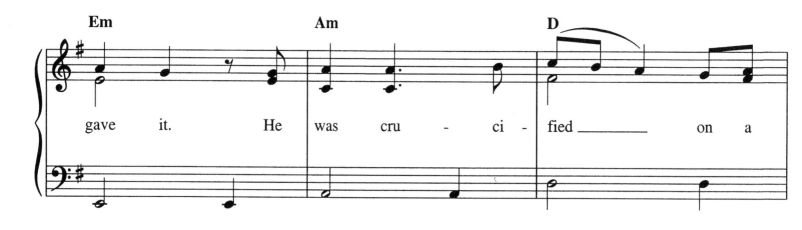

gave it. He was cru - ci - fied _____ on a

tree that He cre - a - ted. ____ Great love for

HE

Words by RICHARD MULLEN
Music by JACK RICHARDS

31

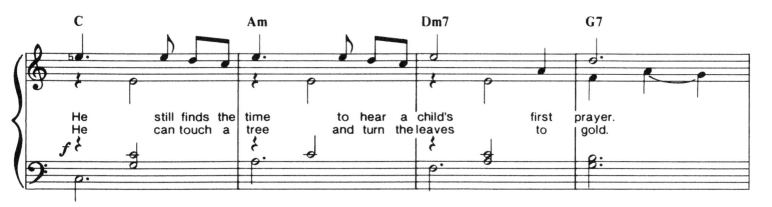

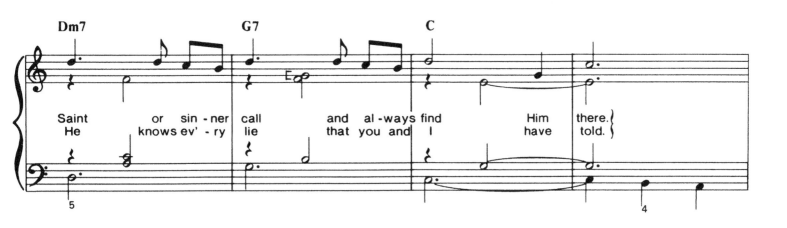

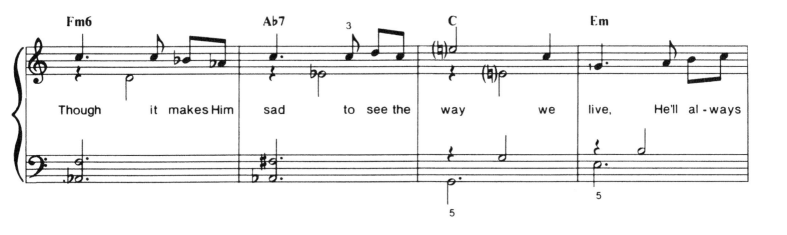

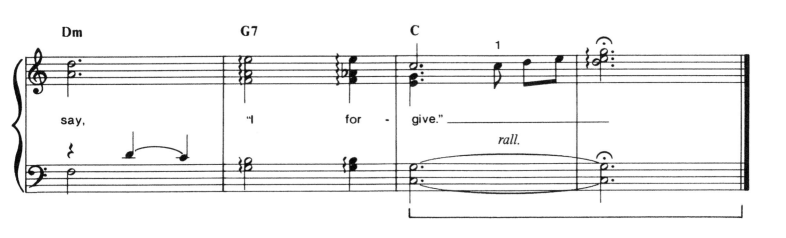

HE LIVES

Words and Music by
A.H. ACKLEY

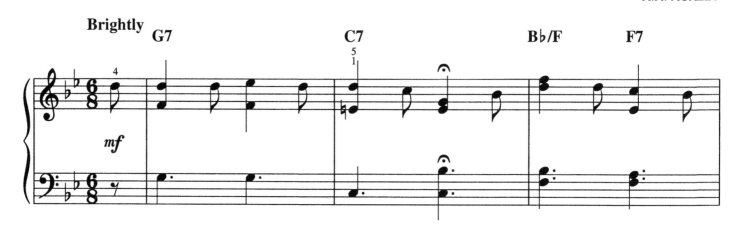

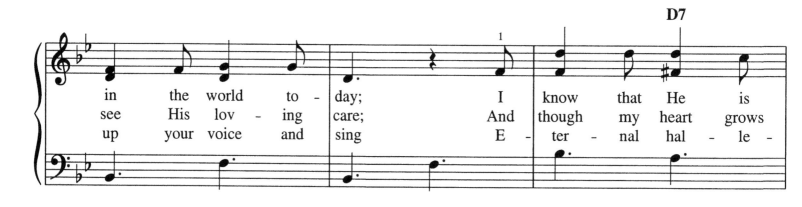

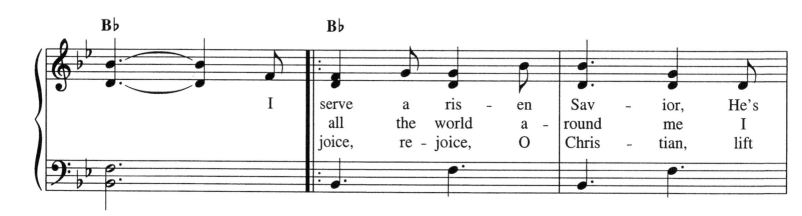

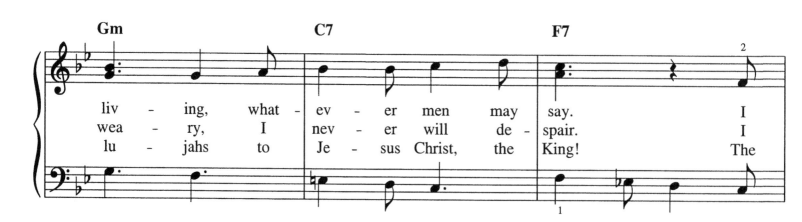

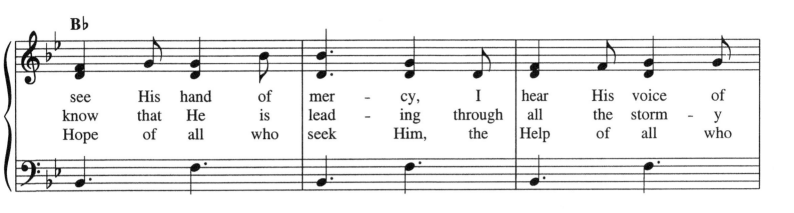

see His hand of mer - cy, I hear His voice of
know that He is lead - ing through all the storm - y
Hope of all who seek Him, the all Help of all who

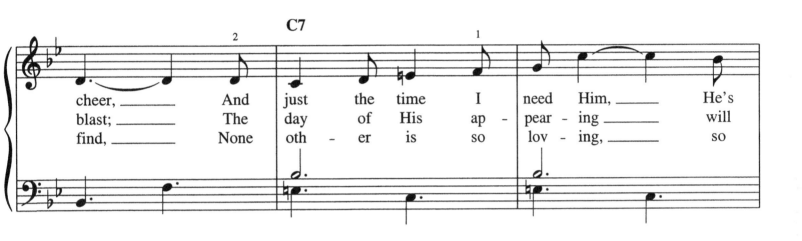

cheer, _____ And just the time I need Him, _____ He's
blast; _____ The day of His ap - pear - ing _____ will
find, _____ None oth - er is so lov - ing, _____ so

al - ways near. _____ } He lives, _____ He lives, _____ Christ
come at last. _____
good and kind. _____

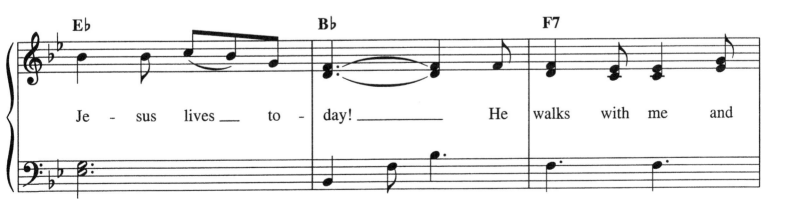

Je - sus lives _____ to - day! _____ He walks with me and

HE LOOKED BEYOND MY FAULT

Words and Music by
DOTTIE RAMBO

With expression

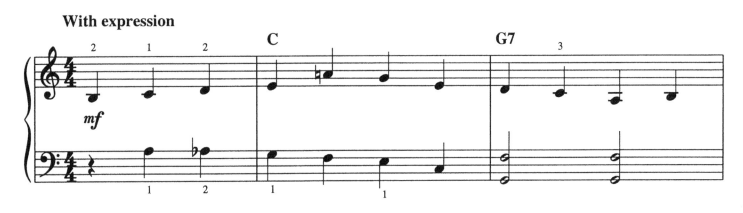

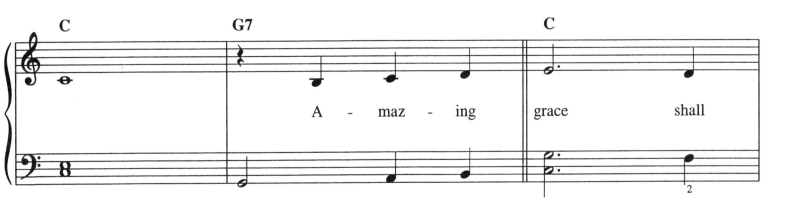

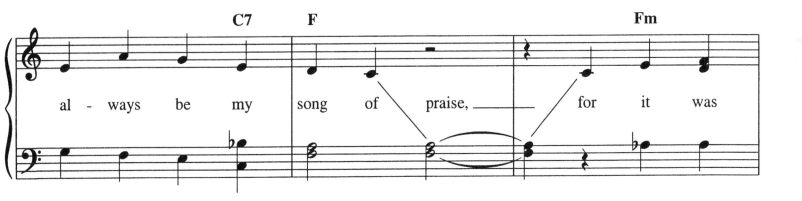

A - maz - ing grace shall al - ways be my song of praise, ___ for it was

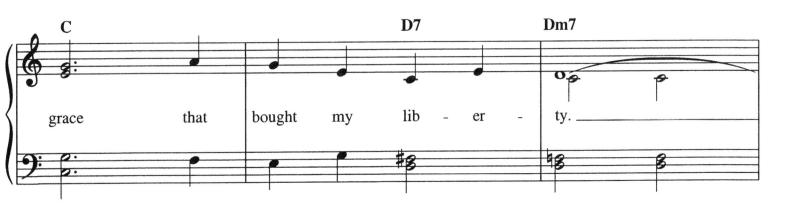

grace that bought my lib - er - ty. ___

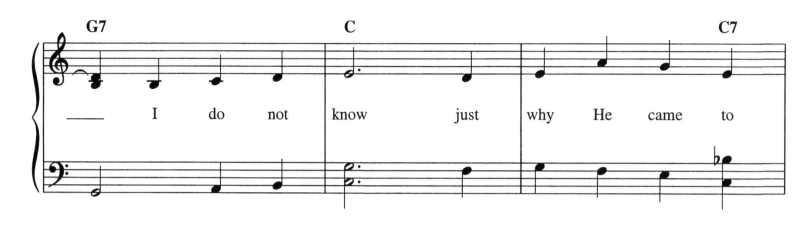

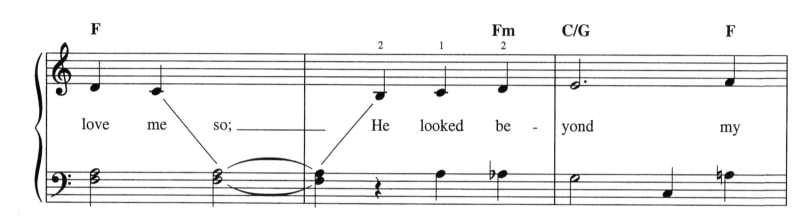

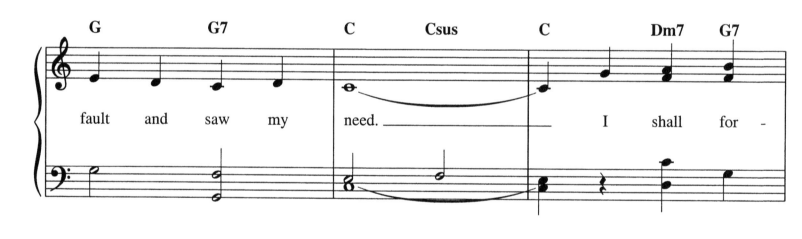

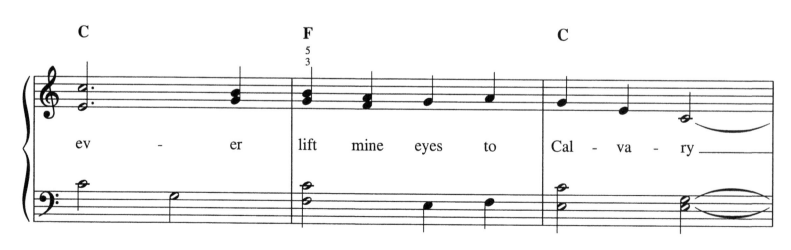

HE TOUCHED ME

Words and Music by
WILLIAM J. GAITHER

Flowing easily

HE'S EVERYTHING TO ME

Words and Music by
RALPH CARMICHAEL

With motion

With pedal

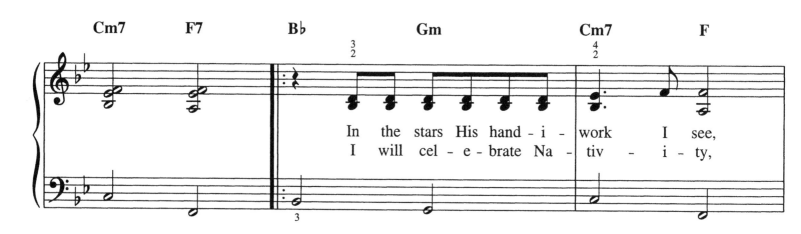

In the stars His hand-i-work I see,
I will cel-e-brate Na-tiv-i-ty,

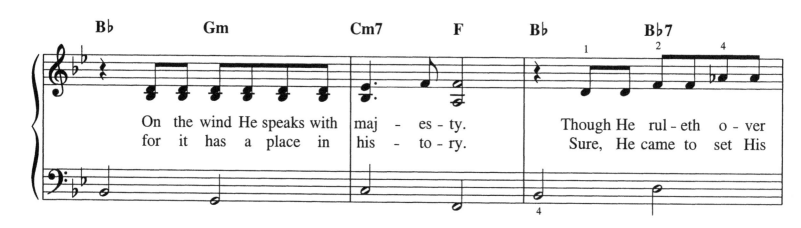

On the wind He speaks with maj-es-ty.
for it has a place in his-to-ry.

Though He rul-eth o-ver
Sure, He came to set His

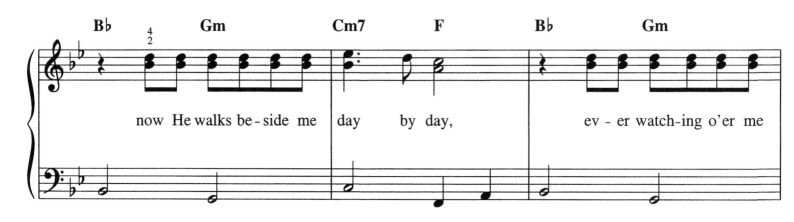

now He walks be - side me day by day, ev - er watch-ing o'er me

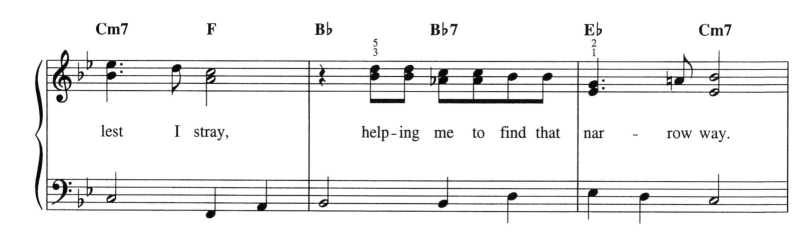

lest I stray, help-ing me to find that nar - row way.

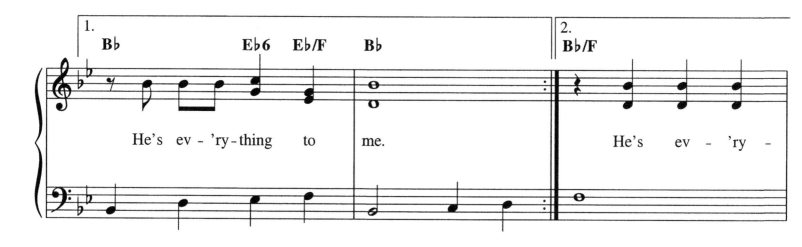

He's ev - 'ry-thing to me. He's ev - 'ry -

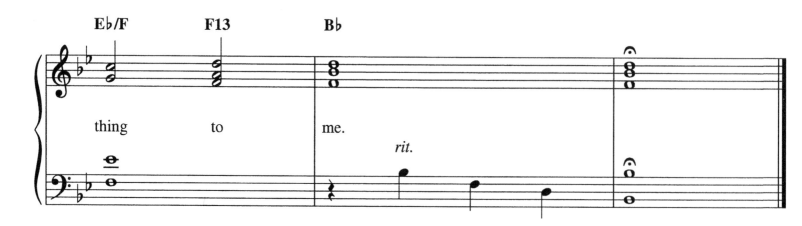

thing to me.

HIS EYE IS ON THE SPARROW

Words by CIVILLA D. MARTIN
Music by CHARLES H. GABRIEL

1. Why should I feel dis-
2. Let not your heart be
3. *(See additional lyrics)*

cour - aged? Why should the shad - ows come?
trou - bled, His ten - der word I hear,

Why should my heart be lone - ly, and long for
And rest - ing on His good - ness, I lose my

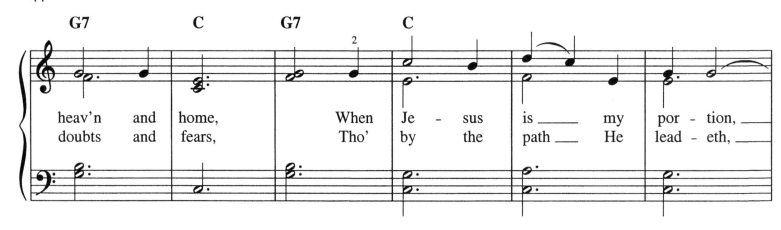

heav'n and home, / doubts and fears, When Je - sus is ____ my por - tion, ____ / Tho' by the path ____ He lead - eth, ____

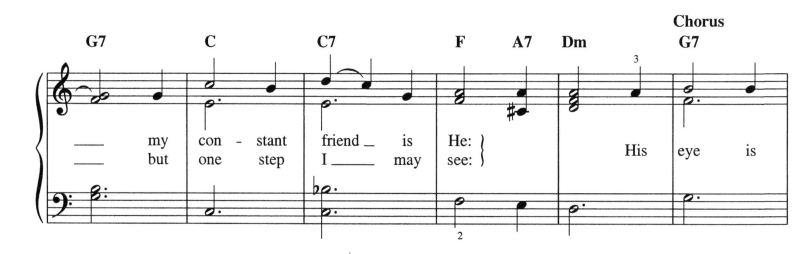

____ my con - stant friend ___ is He: } / ____ but one step I ____ may see: }

Chorus

His eye is

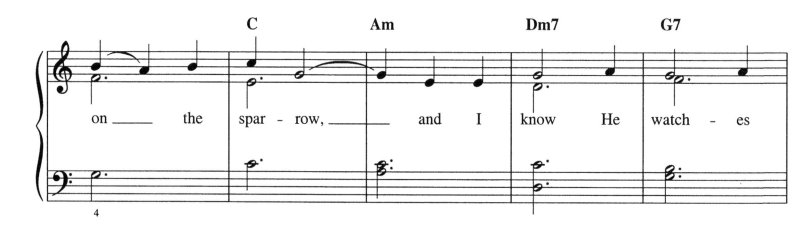

on ____ the spar - row, ____ and I know He watch - es

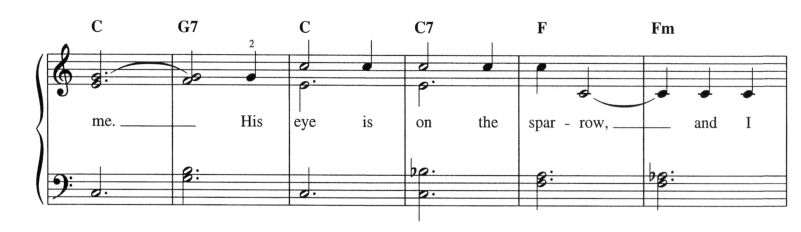

me. ____ His eye is on the spar - row, ____ and I

Additional Lyrics

3. Whenever I am tempted,
   Whenever clouds arise.
   When song gives place to sighing,
   When hope within me dies.
   I draw the closer to Him,
   From care He sets me free:
   Chorus

HE'S GOT THE WHOLE WORLD IN HIS HANDS

Traditional Spiritual

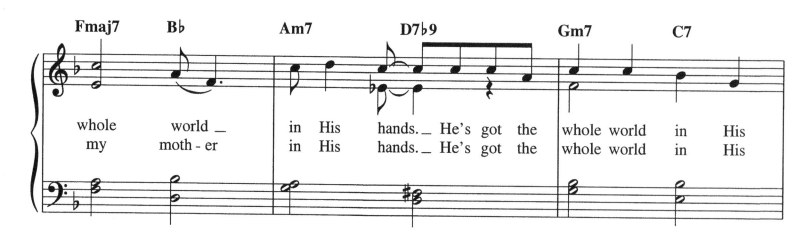

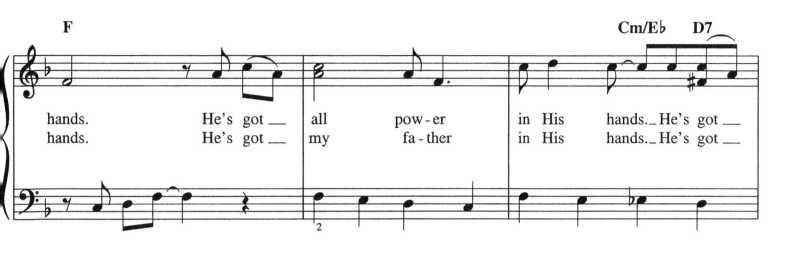

hands. He's got ___ all pow-er in His hands.___ He's got ___
hands. He's got ___ my fa-ther in His hands.___ He's got ___

all pow-er in His hands.___ He's got ___ all pow-er
my fa-ther in His hands.___ He's got ___ my fa-ther

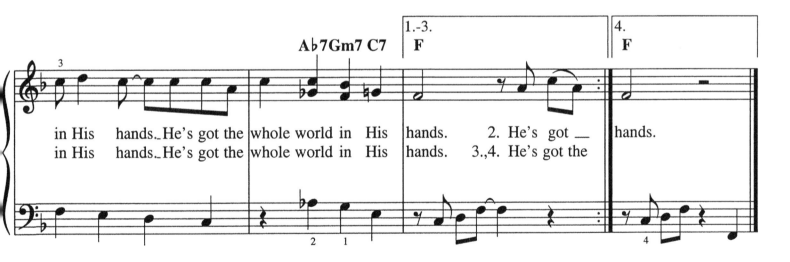

in His hands.___He's got the whole world in His hands. 2. He's got ___ hands.
in His hands.___He's got the whole world in His hands. 3.,4. He's got the

Additional Lyrics

3. He's got the whole church in His hands.
   He's got the whole church in His hands.
   He's got the whole church in His hands.
   He's got the whole world in His hands.

4. He's got the whole world in His hands.
   He's got the whole world in His hands.
   He's got the whole world in His hands.
   He's got the whole world in His hands.

HIS NAME IS WONDERFUL

Words and Music by
AUDREY MIEIR

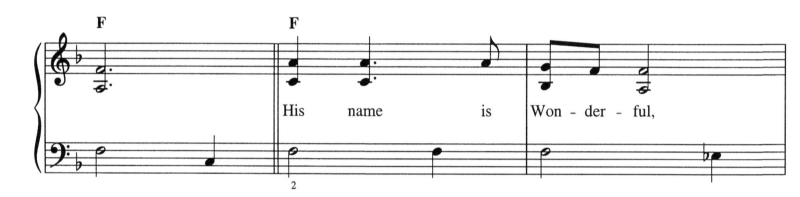

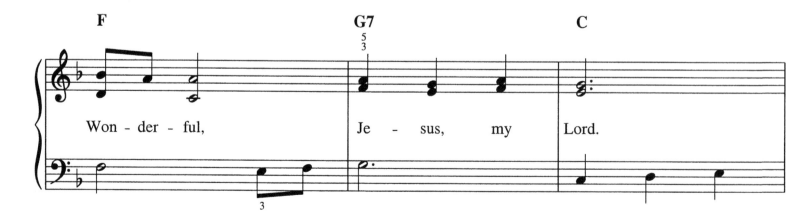

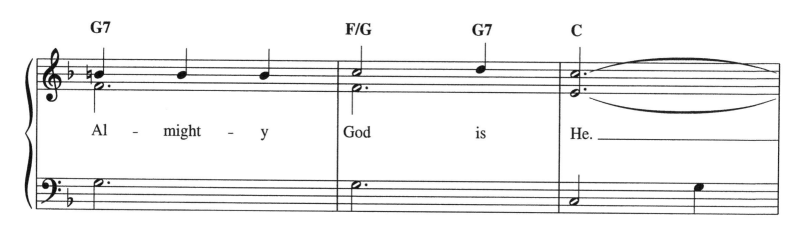

Al - might - y God is He. ____

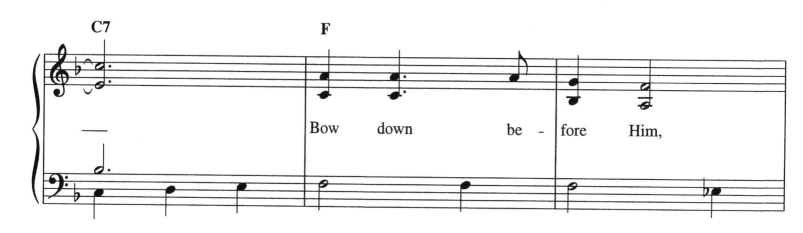

____ Bow down be - fore Him,

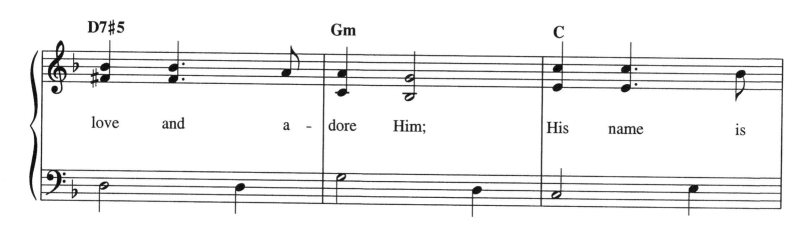

love and a - dore Him; His name is

Won - der - ful, Je - sus, my Lord.

HOW GREAT THOU ART

Words and Music by
STUART K. HINE

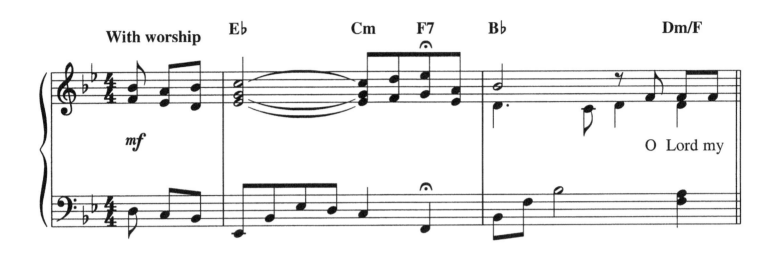

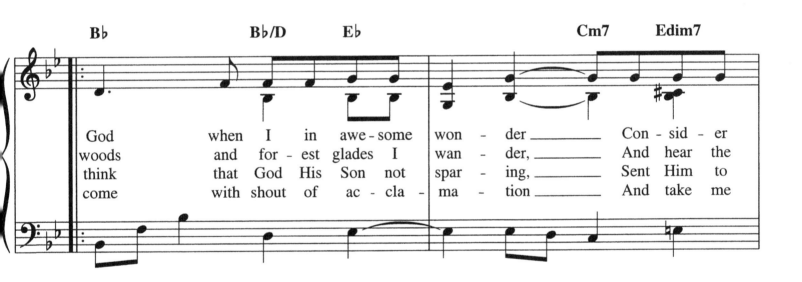

52

I BELIEVE

Words and Music by ERVIN DRAKE, IRVIN GRAHAM,
JIMMY SHIRL and AL STILLMAN

Moderately, with much expression

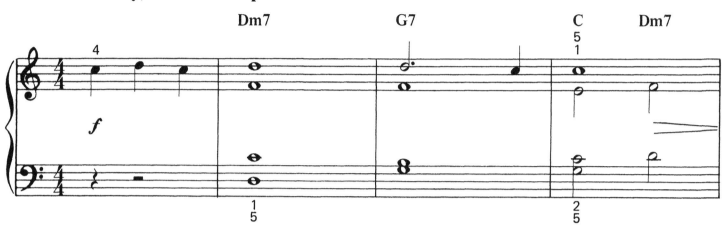

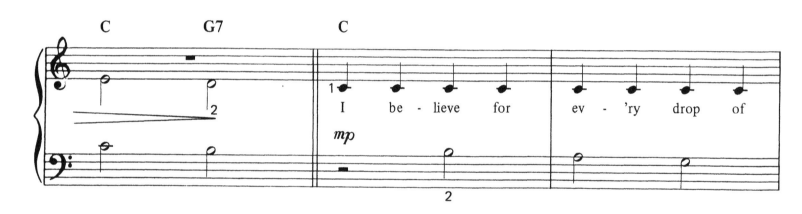

I be - lieve for ev - 'ry drop of

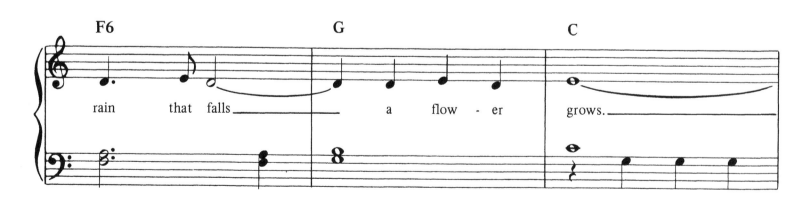

rain that falls _____ a flow - er grows. _____

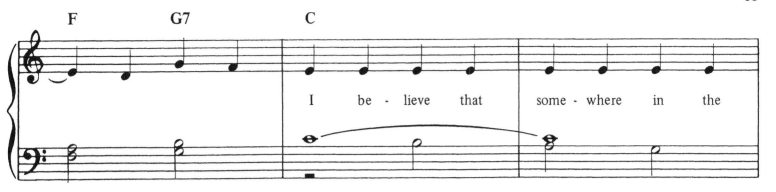

I be - lieve that some - where in the dark - est night _____ a can - dle glows. _____

I be - lieve for ev - 'ry - one who

cresc.

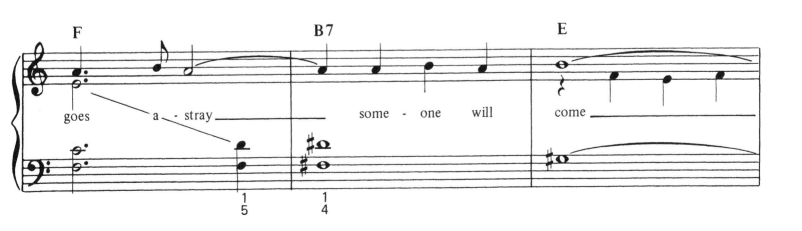

goes a - stray _____ some - one will come _____

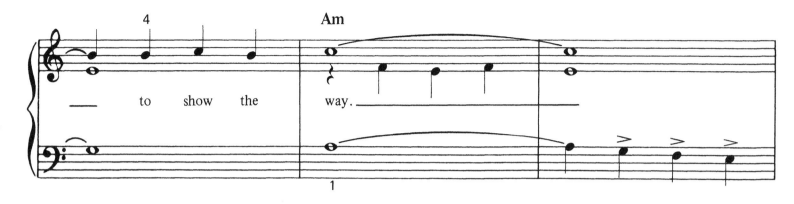

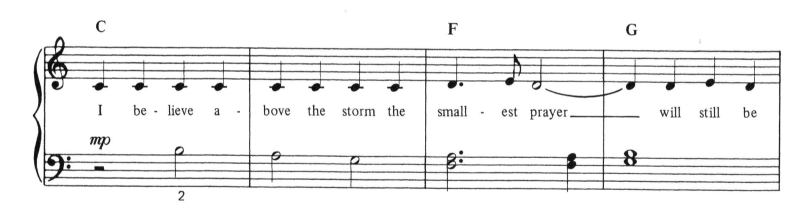

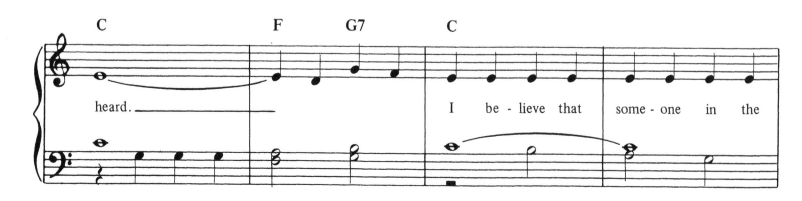

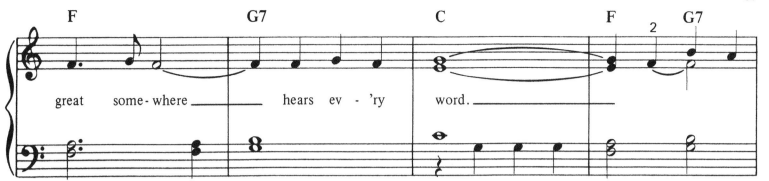

great some-where _____ hears ev - 'ry word. _____

Ev - 'ry time I hear a new - born ba - by cry _____ or touch a

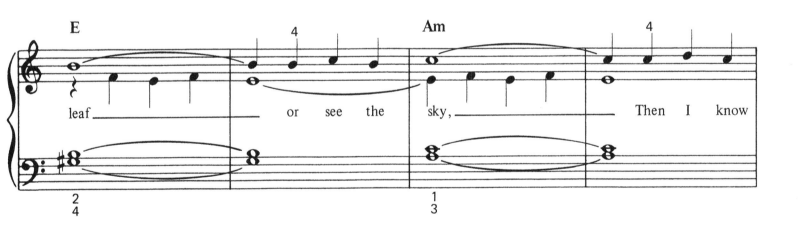

leaf _____ or see the sky, _____ Then I know

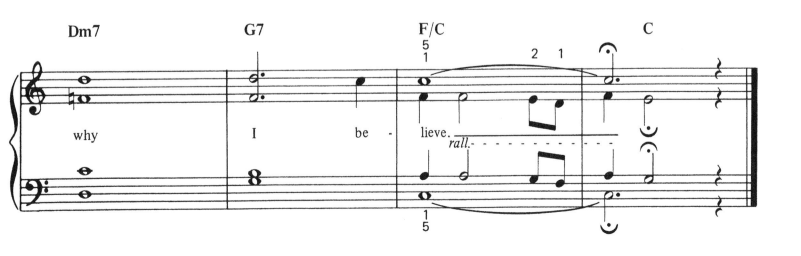

why I be - lieve. _____

I BOWED ON MY KNEES AND CRIED HOLY

Words by NETTIE DUDLEY WASHINGTON
Music by E.M. DUDLEY CANTWELL

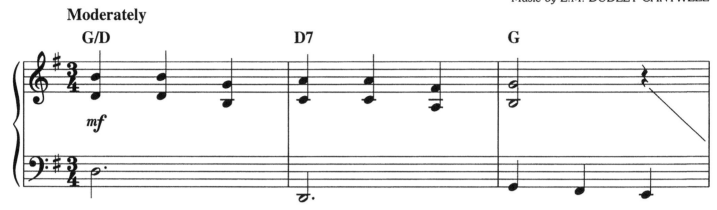

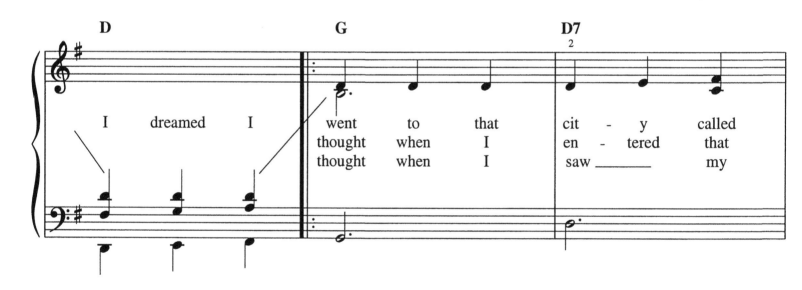

I dreamed I / went to that / cit-y called
thought when I / en-tered that
thought when I / saw _____ my

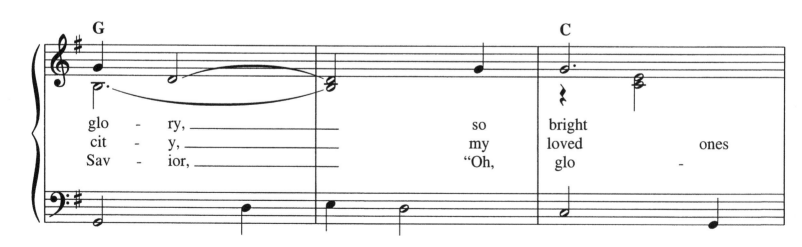

glo - ry, _____ so bright
cit - y, _____ my loved ones
Sav - ior, _____ "Oh, glo -

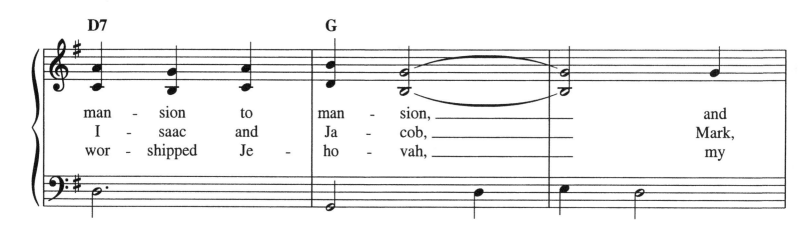

D7   **G**

man - sion   to   man - sion, _____ and
I - saac   and   Ja - cob, _____ Mark,
wor - shipped Je - ho - vah, _____ my

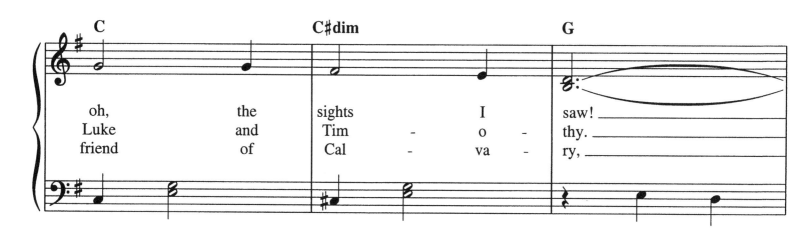

C   **C♯dim**   **G**

oh,   the   sights   I   saw! _____
Luke   and   Tim - o - thy. _____
friend   of   Cal - va - ry, _____

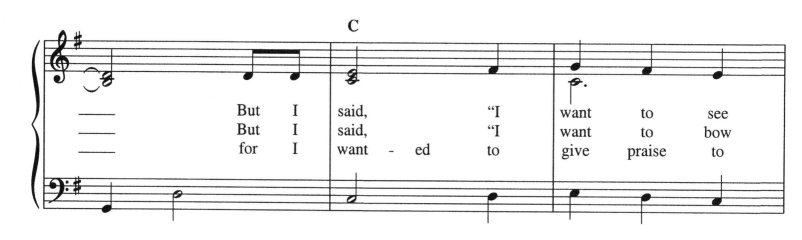

                                    C

_____ But   I   said,   "I   want   to   see
_____ But   I   said,   "I   want   to   bow
_____ for   I   want - ed   to   give   praise   to

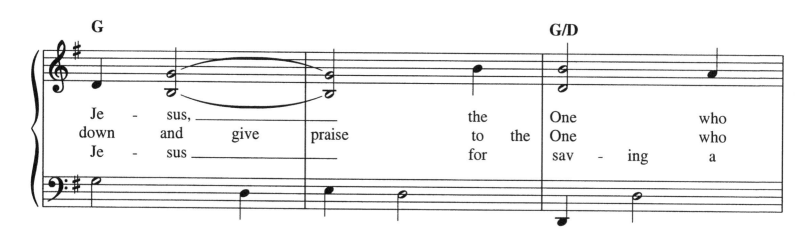

G   **G/D**

Je - sus, _____ the   One   who
down   and   give   praise   to   the   One   who
Je - sus _____ for   sav - ing   a

died   for   all." _____
died   for   me." _____ Then   I
sin - ner   like   me. _____

bowed   on   my   knees   and   cried,   "Ho - ly! _____

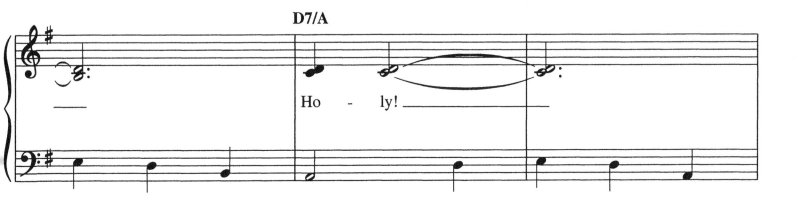

_____ Ho - ly! _____

Ho - ly!" _____ I   clapped   my

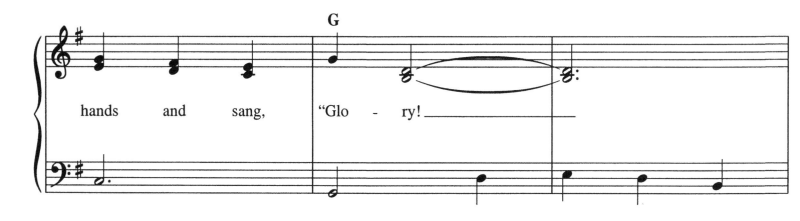

hands and sang, "Glo - ry! _____

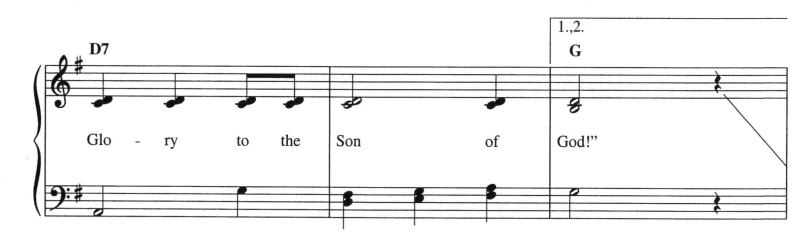

Glo - ry to the Son of God!"

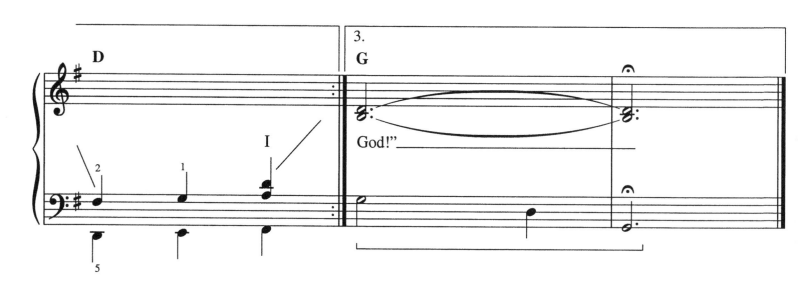

God!" _____

JUST A CLOSER WALK WITH THEE

Traditional
Arranged by KENNETH MORRIS

64

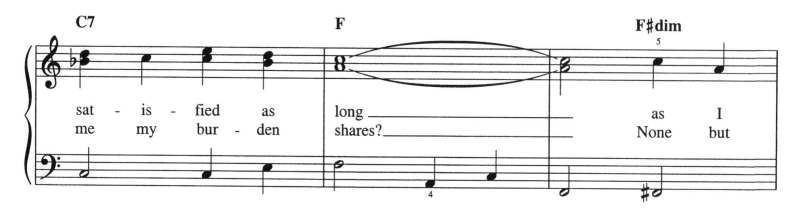

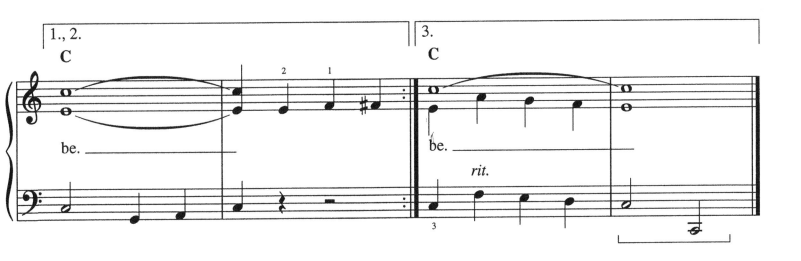

Additional Verse

3. When my feeble life is o'er,
   Time for me will be no more.
   Guide me gently, safely o'er
   To Thy kingdom shore, to Thy shore.

I SAW THE LIGHT

Words and Music by
HANK WILLIAMS

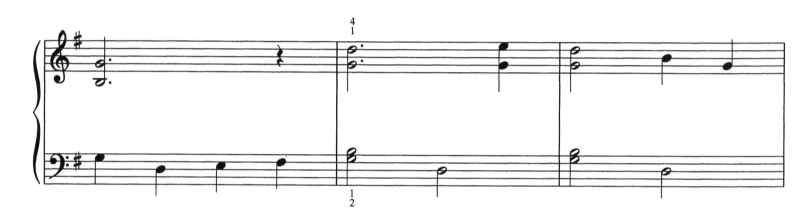

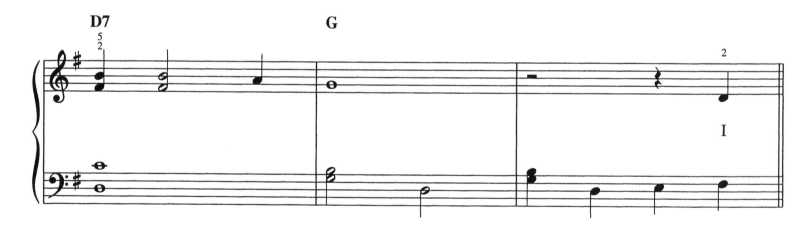

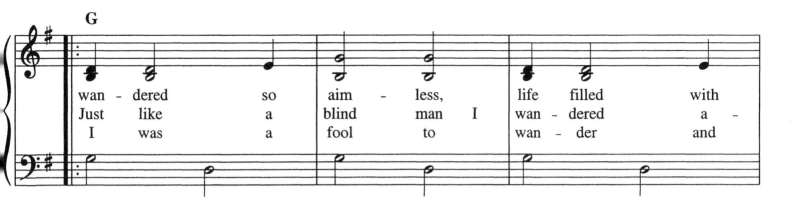

G

wan - dered   so   aim - less,   life   filled   with
Just   like   a   blind   man   I   wan - dered   a -
I   was   a   fool   to   wan - der   and

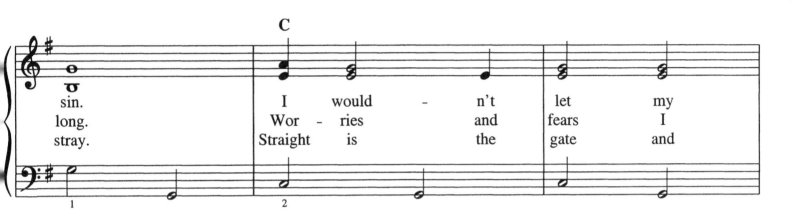

C

sin.
long.   Wor - ries   and   fears   I
stray.   Straight   is   the   gate   and
I   would - n't   let   my

1   2

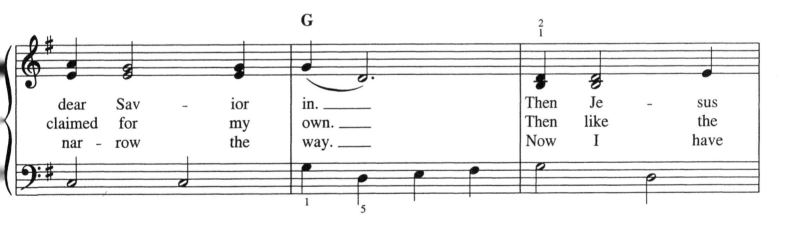

G

2
1

dear   Sav - ior   in. ____
claimed   for   my   own. ____   Then   Je - sus
nar - row   the   way. ____   Then   like   the
Now   I   have

1   5

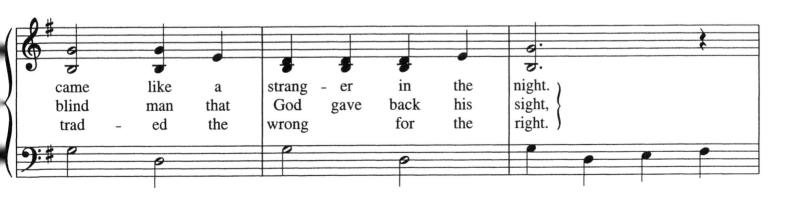

came   like   a   strang - er   in   the   night.)
blind   man   that   God   gave   back   for   his   sight, }
trad - ed   the   wrong   for   the   right.)

68

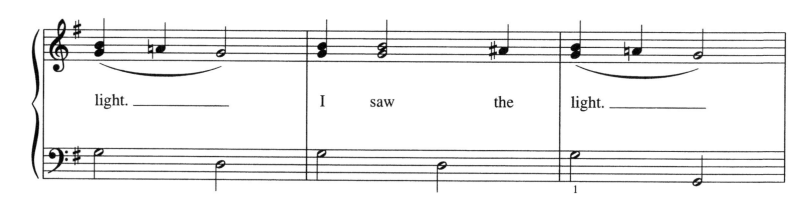

I'LL FLY AWAY

Words and Music by
ALBERT E. BRUMLEY

Brightly

F   Gm7   F/A   C7

mf

F   A7

Some glad morn - ing when this life is o'er, _____
Just a few more wea - ry days and then, _____

Bb   Gm7   Bb/C   F   Bb   C   F

I'll   fly a - way.   To a home on
I'll   fly a - way.   To a land where

A   A7   Dm   Gm9   C7

God's ce - les - tial shore,   I'll   fly a -
joy shall nev - er end,   I'll   fly a -

IN THE GARDEN

Words and Music by
C. AUSTIN MILES

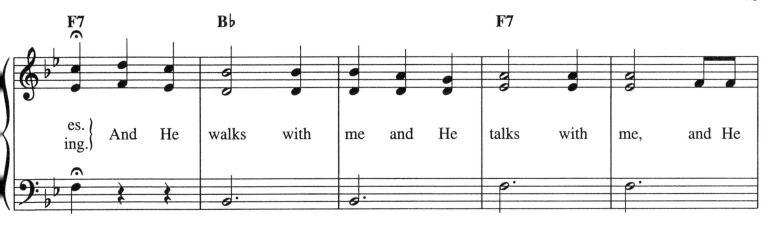

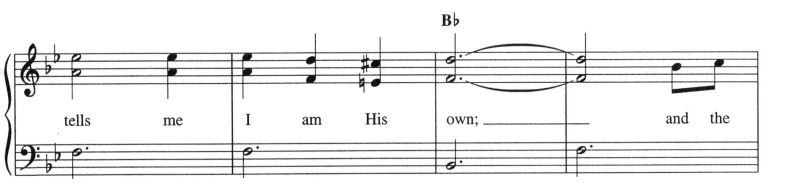

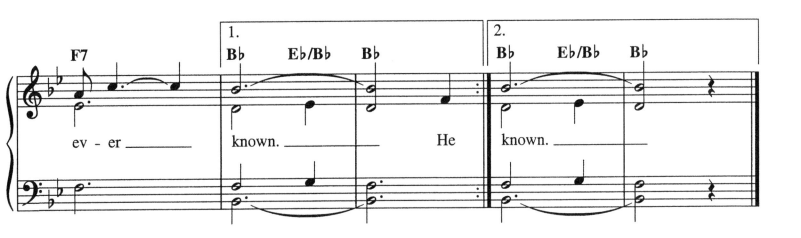

JUST AS I AM

Words by CHARLOTTE ELLIOTT
Music by WILLIAM B. BRADBURY

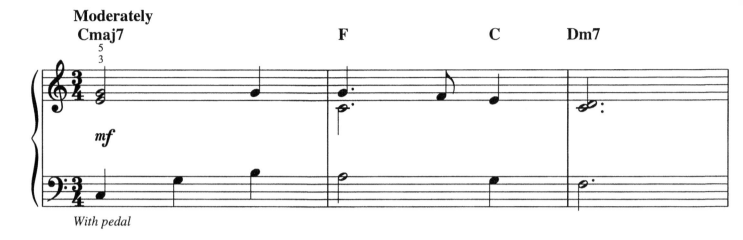

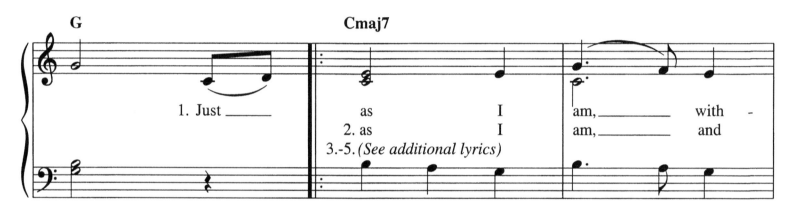

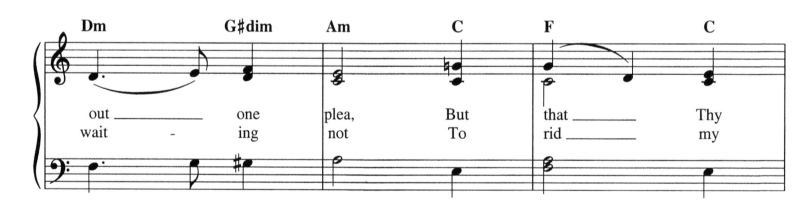

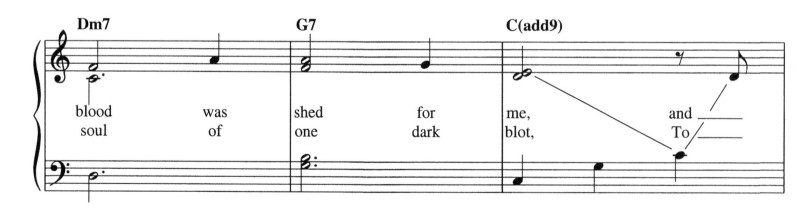

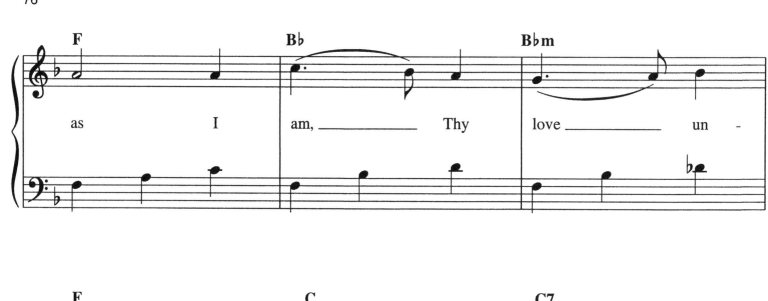

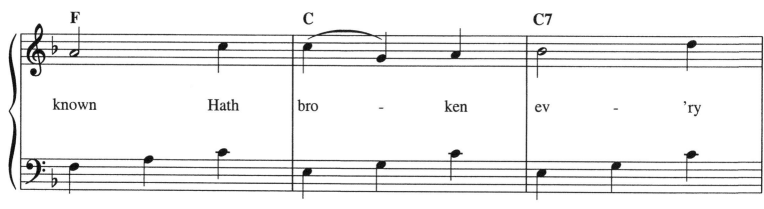

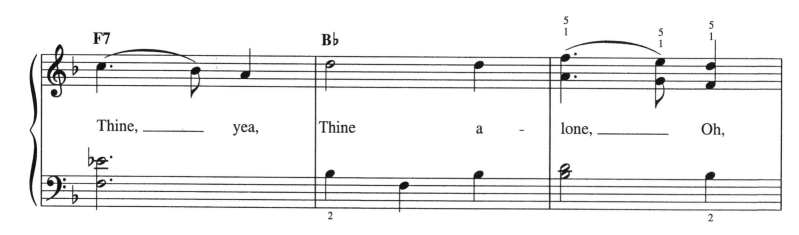

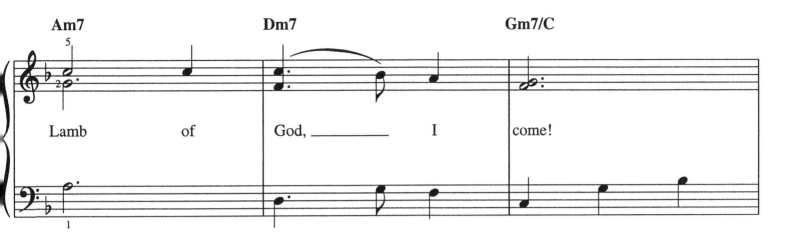

Lamb of God, _____ I come!

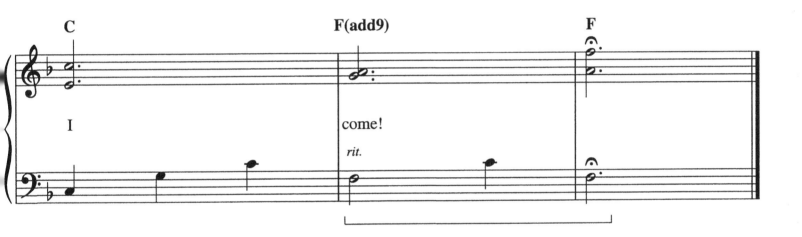

I come!

rit.

Additional Lyrics

3. Just as I am, tho' tossed about
   With many a conflict, many a doubt,
   Fightings within and fears without,
   Oh, Lamb of God, I come! I come!

4. Just as I am, poor, wretched, blind;
   Sight, riches, healing of the mind,
   Yea, all I need in Thee to find,
   Oh, Lamb of God, I come! I come!

5. Just as I am, Thou wilt receive,
   Wilt welcome, pardon, cleanse, relieve,
   Because Thy promise I believe,
   Oh, Lamb of God, I come! I come!

THE KING IS COMING

Words by WILLIAM J. and GLORIA GAITHER
and CHARLES MILLHUFF
Music by WILLIAM J. GAITHER

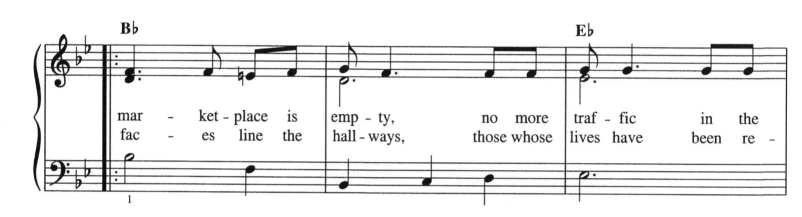

The mar- ket- place is emp- ty, no more traf- fic in the
fac- es line the hall- ways, those whose lives have been re-

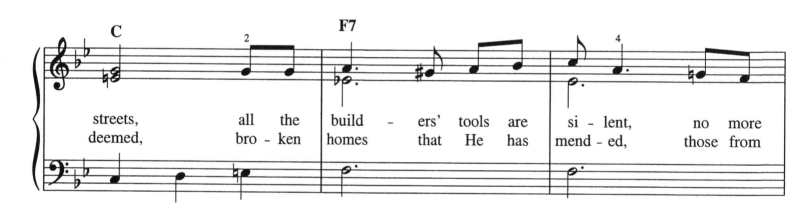

streets, all the build- ers' tools are si- lent, no more
deemed, bro- ken homes that He has mend- ed, those from

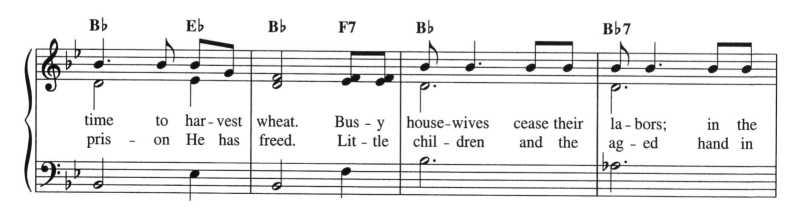

time to har- vest wheat. Bus- y house- wives cease their la- bors; in the
pris- on He has freed. Lit- tle chil- dren and the ag- ed hand in

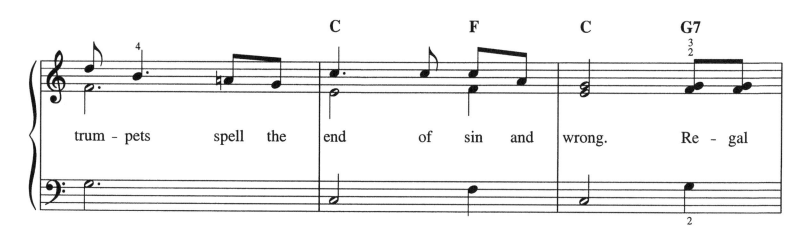

trum - pets spell the | end of sin and | wrong. Re - gal

robes are now un - | fold-ing, Heav-en's | grand - stands all in | place, Heav-en's

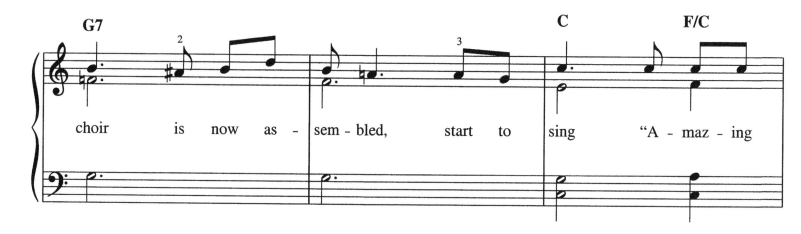

choir is now as - | sem - bled, start to sing | "A - maz - ing

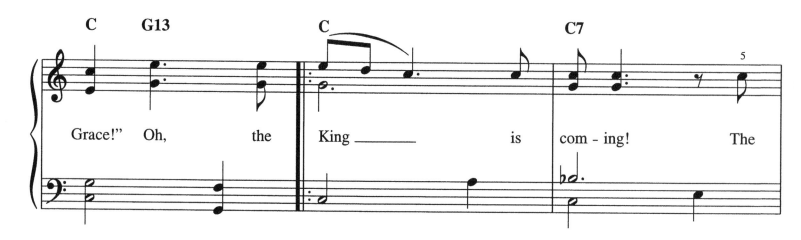

Grace!" Oh, the | King _____ is com - ing! | The

KUM BA YAH

Traditional Spiritual

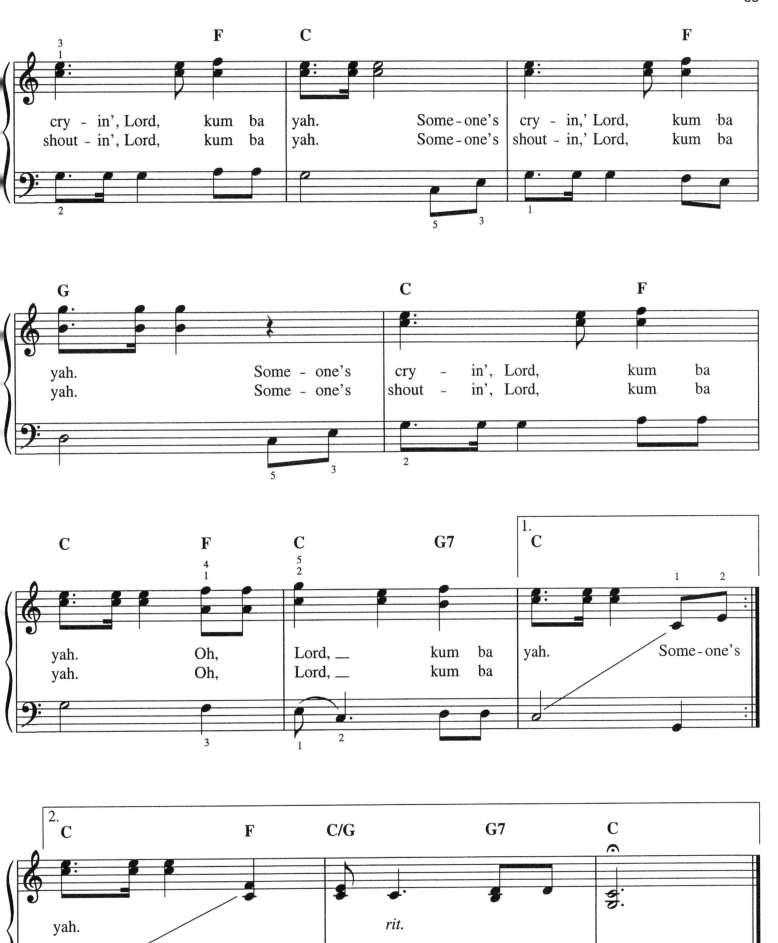

LEAD ME, GUIDE ME

Words and Music by
DORIS AKERS

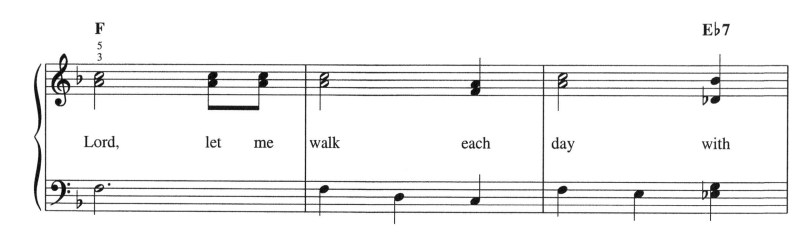

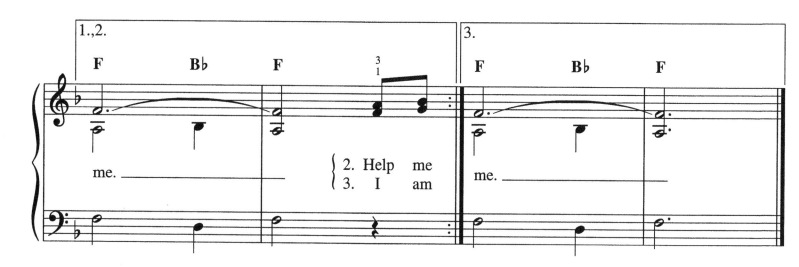

Additional Lyrics

3. I am lost if You take Your hand from me.
   I am blind without Thy light to see.
   Lord, just always let me Thy servant be.
   Lead me, oh Lord, lead me.
   Chorus

THE OLD RUGGED CROSS

Words and Music by
REV. GEORGE BENNARD

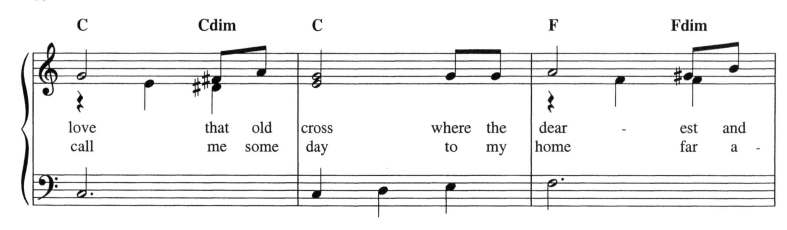

love that old cross
call me some day

where the dear - est and
to my home far a -

best for a world of lost sin - ners was
way, where this glo - ry for - ev - er I'll

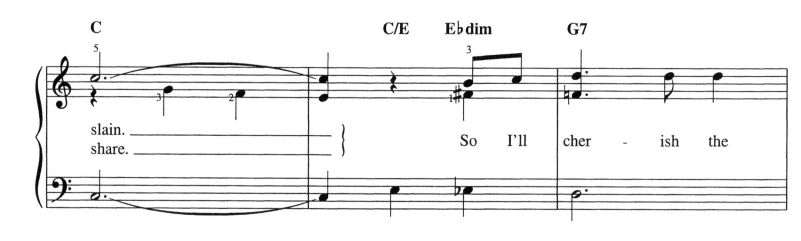

slain. _____
share. _____

So I'll cher - ish the

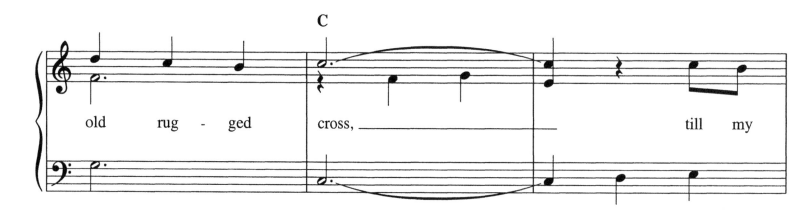

old rug - ged cross, _____ till my

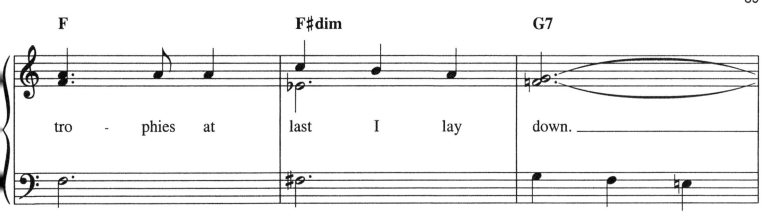

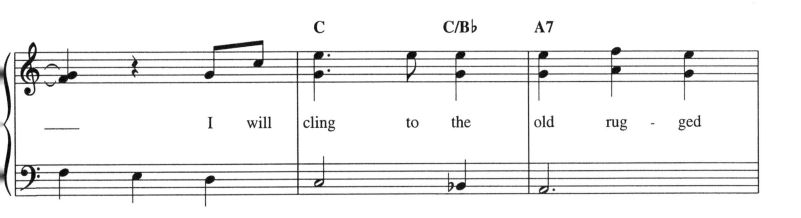

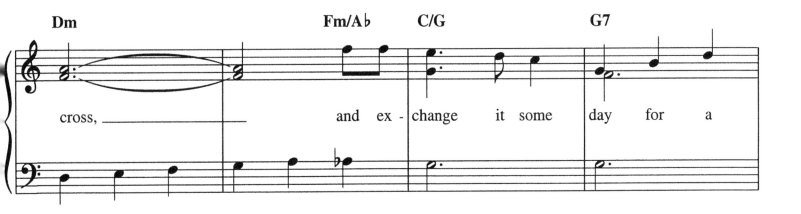

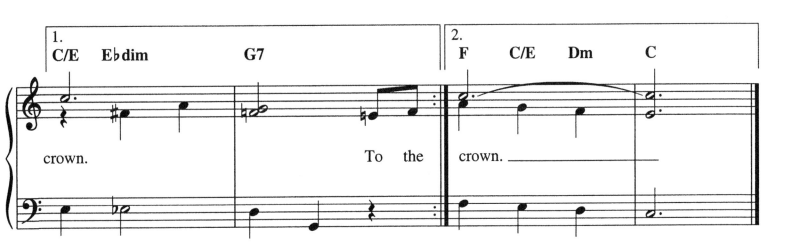

MY GOD IS REAL

(Yes, God Is Real)

Words and Music by
KENNETH MORRIS

There are some

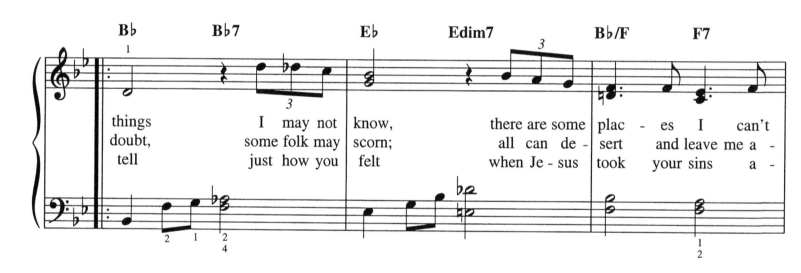

things / doubt, / tell   I may not / some folk may / just how you   know, / scorn; / felt   there are some / all can de- / when Je-sus   plac-es I can't / sert and leave me a- / took your sins a-

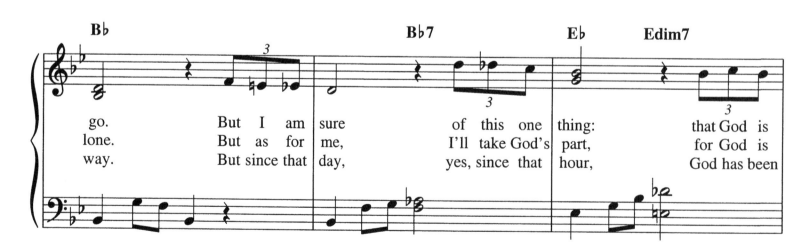

go. / lone. / way.   But I am / But as for / But since that   sure / me, / day,   of this one / I'll take God's / yes, since that   thing: / part, / hour,   that God is / for God is / God has been

MY TRIBUTE

Words and Music by
ANDRAÉ CROUCH

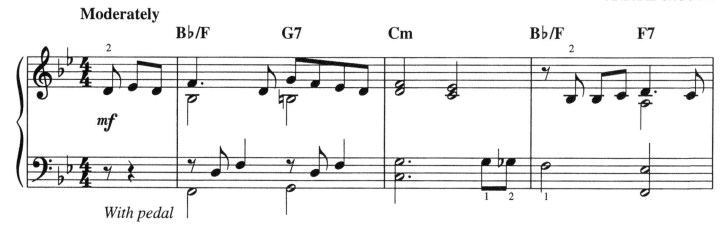

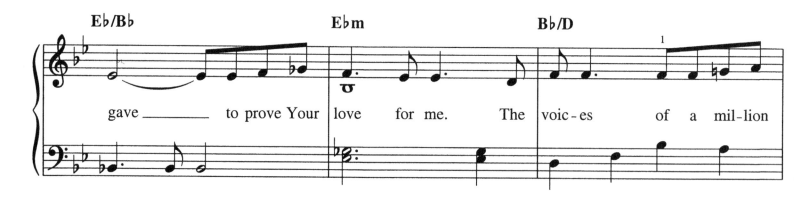

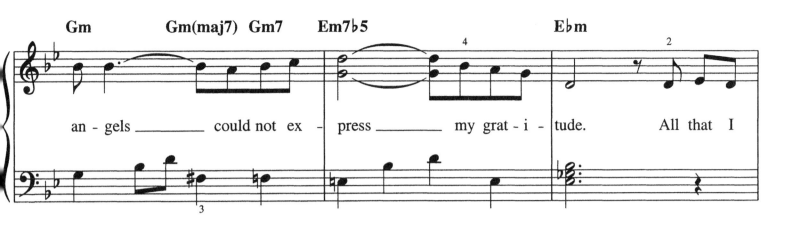

an - gels _____ could not ex - press _____ my grat - i - tude. All that I

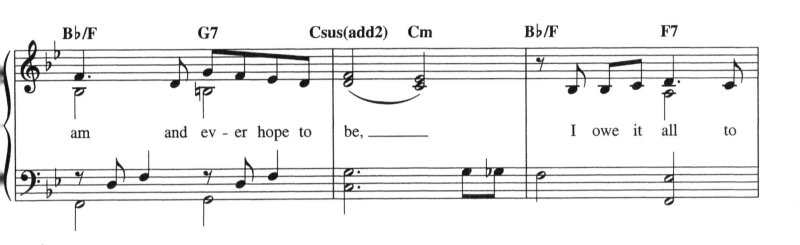

am and ev - er hope to be, _____ I owe it all to

Thee. To God be the glo - ry, to God be the

glo - ry, to God be the glo - ry for the

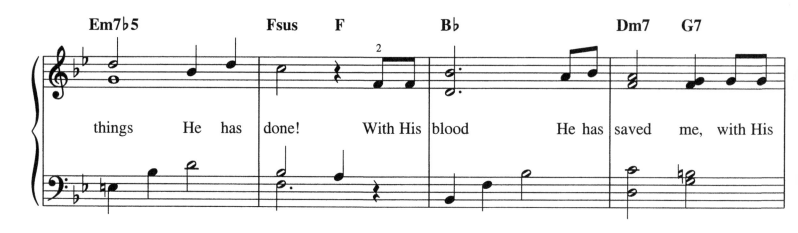

things He has done! With His blood He has saved me, with His

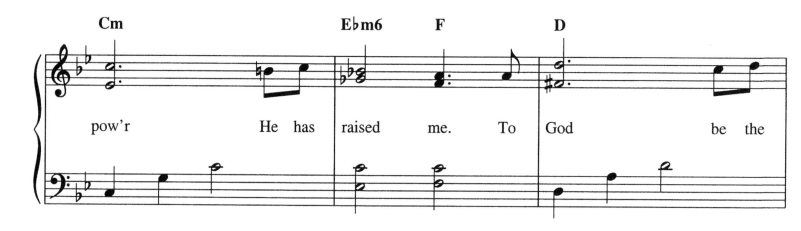

pow'r He has raised me. To God be the

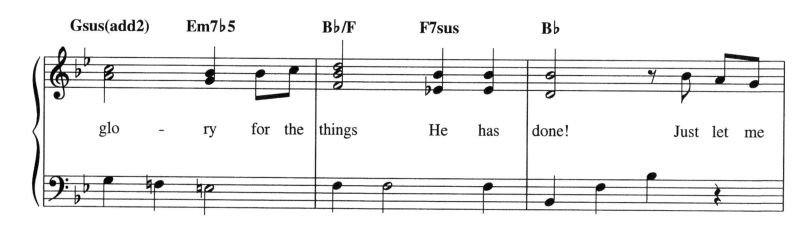

glo - ry for the things He has done! Just let me

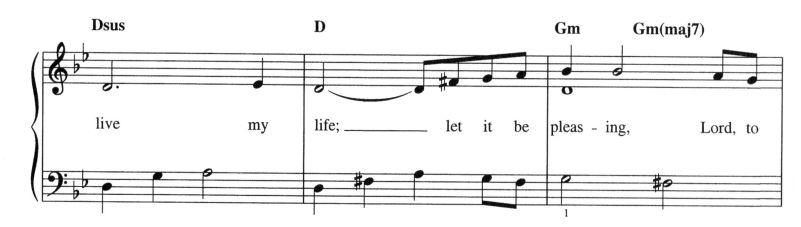

live my life; _____ let it be pleas - ing, Lord, to

OVER THE NEXT HILL WE'LL BE HOME

Words and Music by
JOHN R. CASH

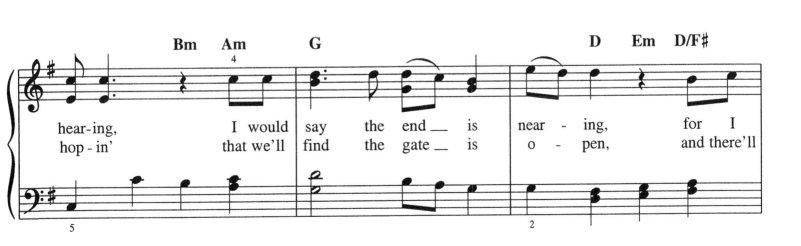

see fa-mil-iar | land-marks all a - long. | | By the
be a ref-uge | from _ the com-ing | storm. | | For the

dreams that I've been | dream-ing, there will | be a great re -
way's been long and | wea-ry, but at | last the end is

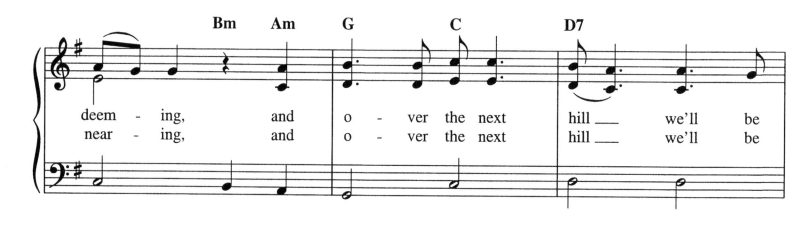

deem - ing, and | o - ver the next | hill ___ we'll be
near - ing, and | o - ver the next | hill ___ we'll be

home. ___ | | By the | home. ___

(There'll Be)
PEACE IN THE VALLEY
(For Me)

Words and Music by
THOMAS A. DORSEY

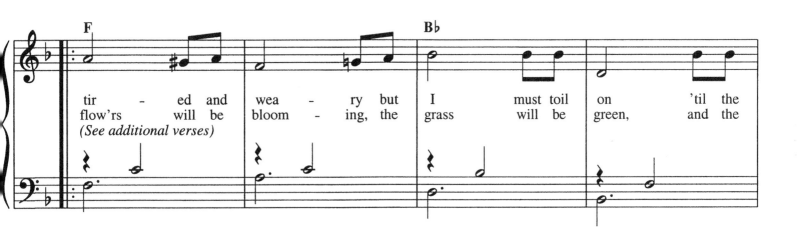

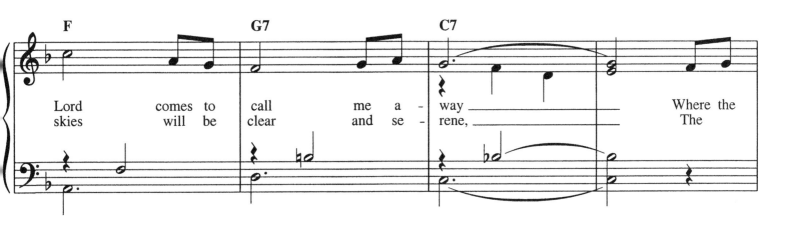

100

morn - ing is bright, and the Lamb is the light and the
sun ev - er shines, giv - ing one is end-less beam and no

night is as fair as the day. ___ There'll be
clouds there will ev - er be seen. ___

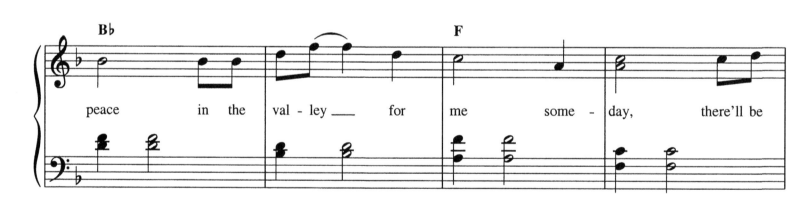

peace in the val - ley ___ for me some - day, there'll be

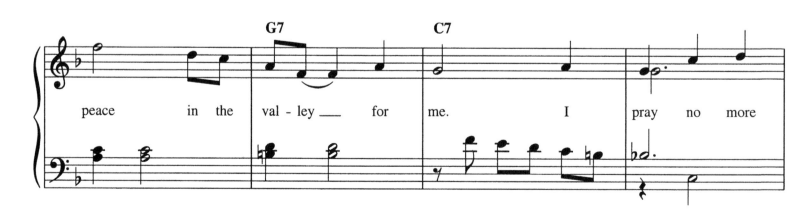

peace in the val - ley ___ for me. I pray no more

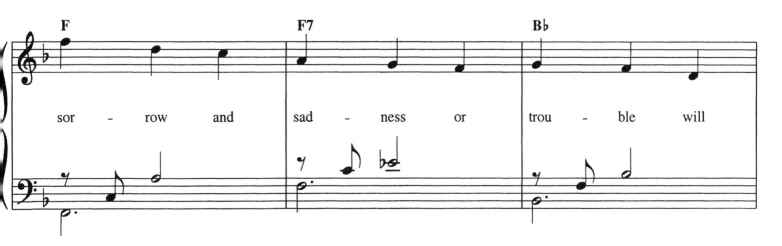

sor - row and sad - ness or trou - ble will

be, there'll be peace _____ in the val - ley _____ for

1-3

me. _____ There the me. _____

Additional Verses

(3.) There the bear will be gentle, the wolf will be tame,
And the lion will lay down with the lamb.
The host from the wild will be led by a Child,
I'll be changed from the creature I am.

(4.) No headaches or heartaches or misunderstands,
No confusion or trouble won't be.
No frowns to defile, just a big endless smile,
There'll be peace and contentment for me.

PRECIOUS LORD, TAKE MY HAND

(Take My Hand, Precious Lord)

Words and Music by
THOMAS A. DORSEY

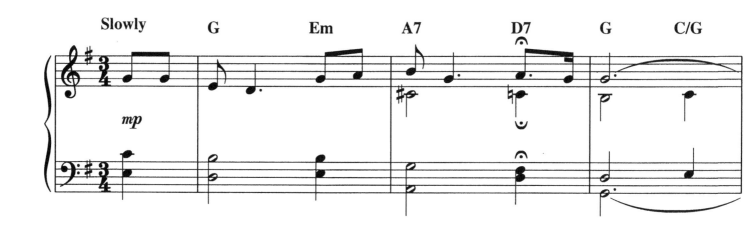

Pre-cious Lord take my hand, lead me on, let me

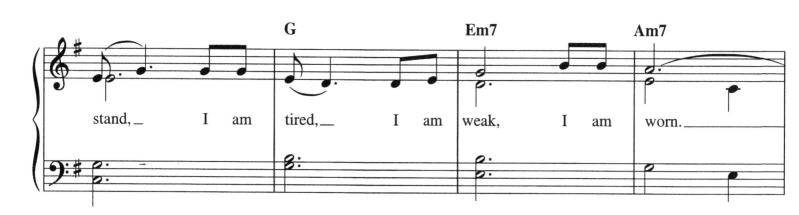

stand, __ I am tired, __ I am weak, I am worn. __

SING YOUR PRAISE TO THE LORD

Words and Music by
RICHARD MULLINS

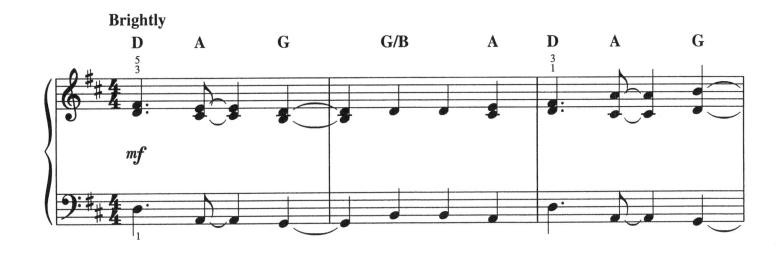

Sing your praise to the Lord, come on ev-'ry-bod-y,

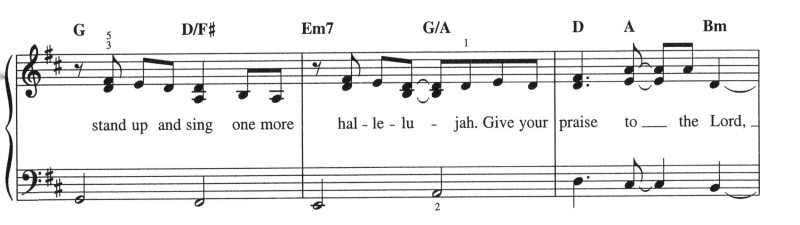

stand up and sing one more hal-le-lu-jah. Give your praise to the Lord,

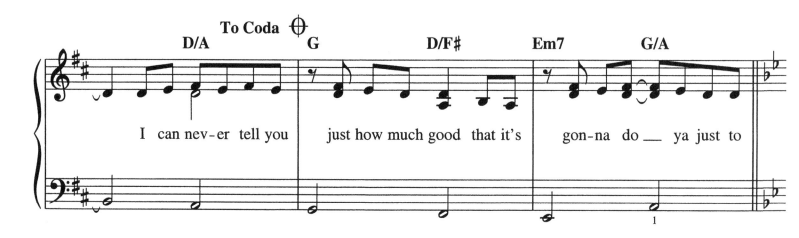

To Coda ⊕

D/A G D/F# Em7 G/A

I can nev-er tell you | just how much good that it's | gon-na do __ ya just to

Bb Eb/Bb F/Bb

sing a - new | the song your heart __ learned to
sing a - loud | the song that some - one is

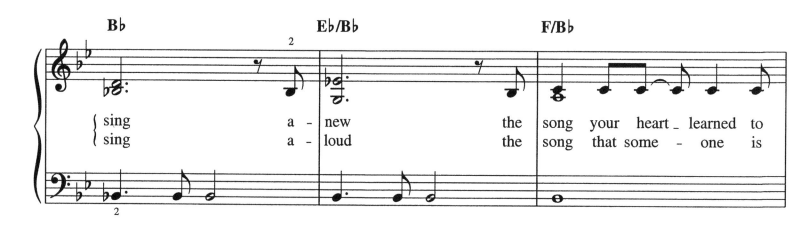

Eb/Bb Bb Eb/Bb

sing when He __ first gave His | life to you, | the
dy- ing to hear __ down in the | mad - d'ning crowd | as

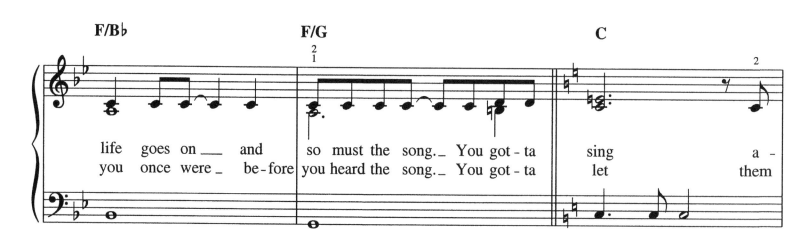

F/Bb F/G C

life goes on ___ and | so must the song.__ You got - ta | sing a -
you once were __ be-fore | you heard the song.__ You got - ta | let them

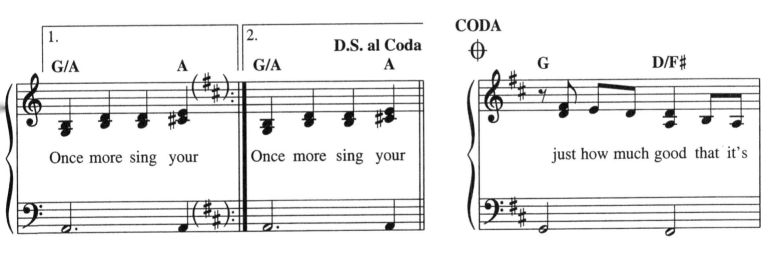

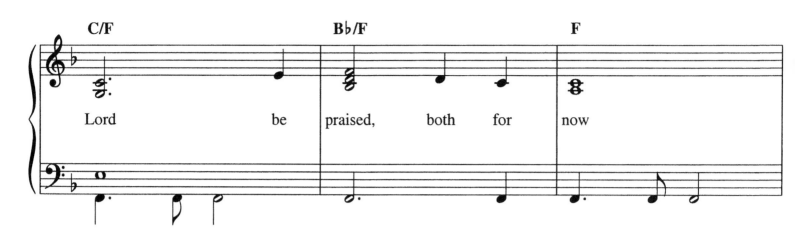

Lord be praised, both for now

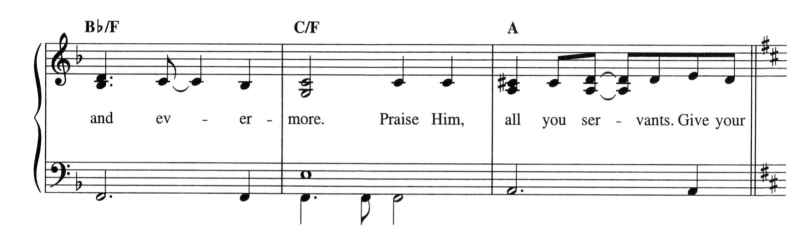

and ev - er - more. Praise Him, all you ser - vants. Give your

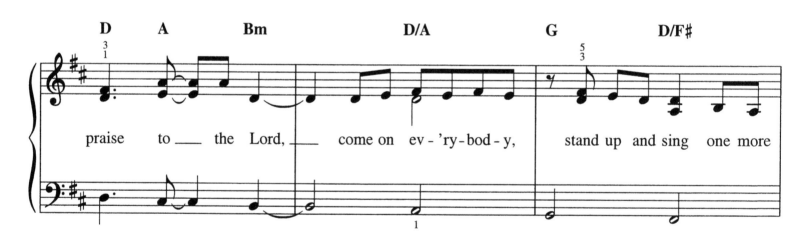

praise to ___ the Lord, ___ come on ev - 'ry - bod - y, stand up and sing one more

hal - le - lu - jah. Give your praise to ___ the Lord, I can nev - er tell you

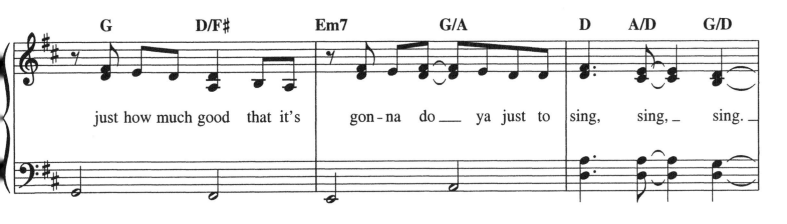

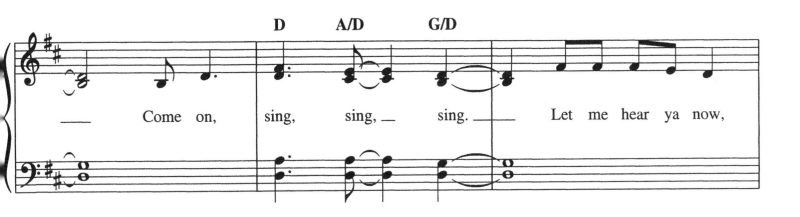

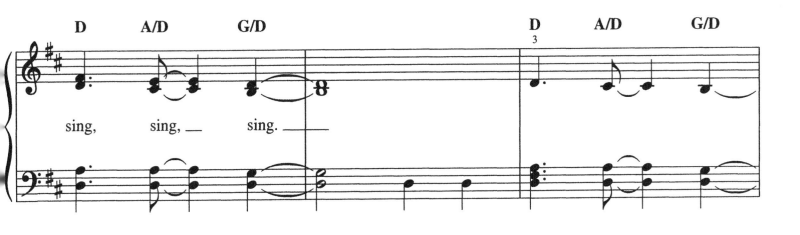

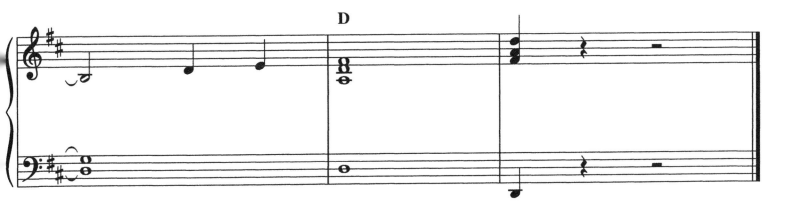

PRECIOUS MEMORIES

Words and Music by
J.B.F. WRIGHT

Moderately slow

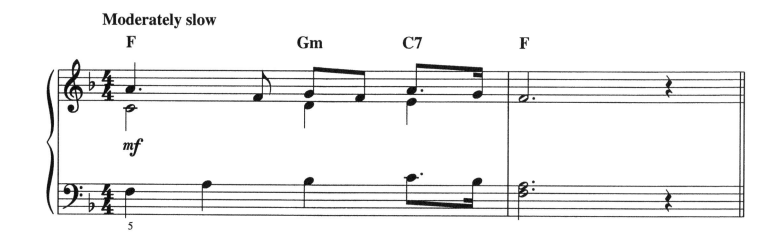

Pre - cious mem - 'ries,   un -   seen an - gels
Pre - cious fa - ther,   lov - ing moth - er

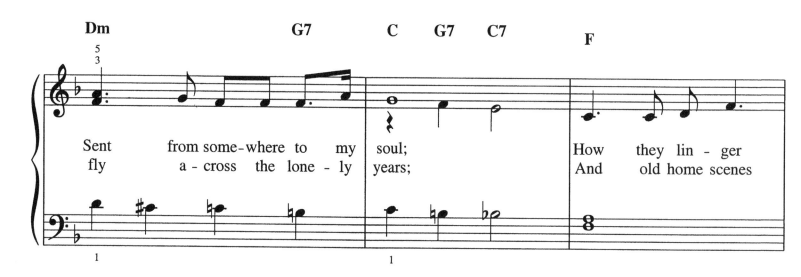

Sent   from some-where to   my   soul;   How   they lin - ger
fly   a - cross the lone - ly   years;   And   old home scenes

PUT YOUR HAND IN THE HAND

Words and Music by
GENE MacLELLAN

Moderately, with a beat

Put your hand in the hand of the Man who stilled the

wa - ter, put your hand in the hand of the

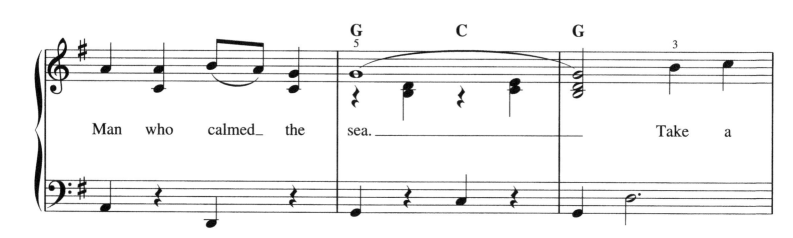

Man who calmed the sea. Take a

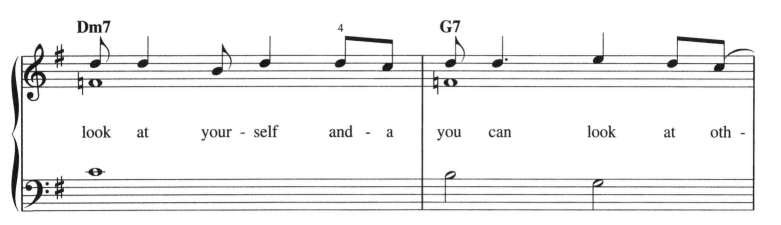

look at your-self and - a you can look at oth-

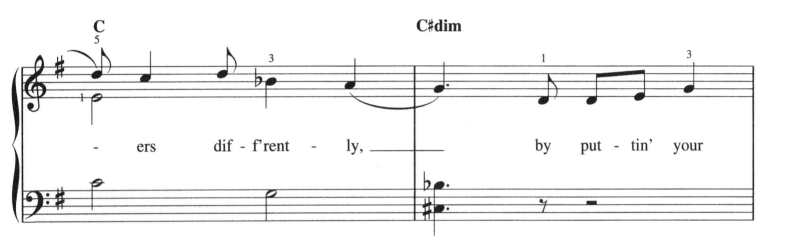

-ers dif - f'rent - ly, _____ by put - tin' your

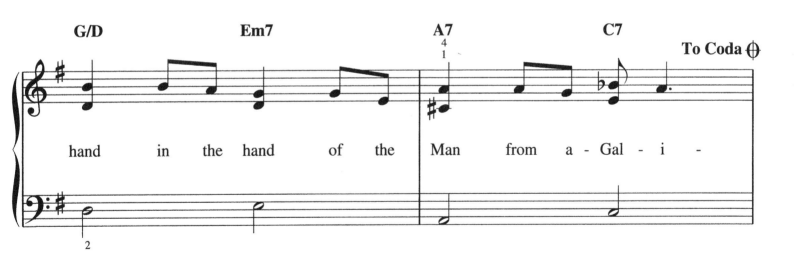

hand in the hand of the Man from a - Gal - i -

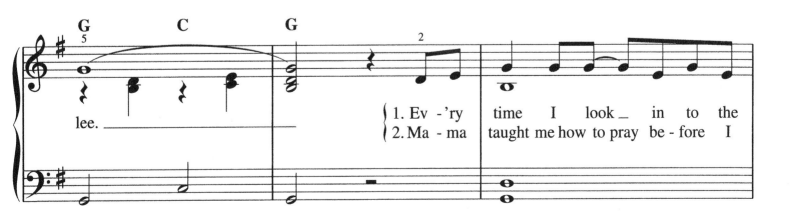

lee. _____

1. Ev -'ry time I look _ in to the
2. Ma - ma taught me how to pray be - fore I

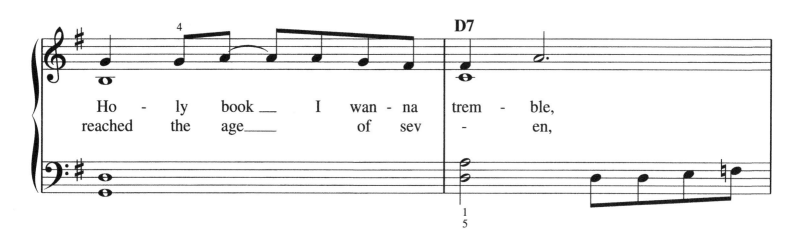

Ho - ly book __ I wan - na trem - ble,
reached the age ___ of sev - en,

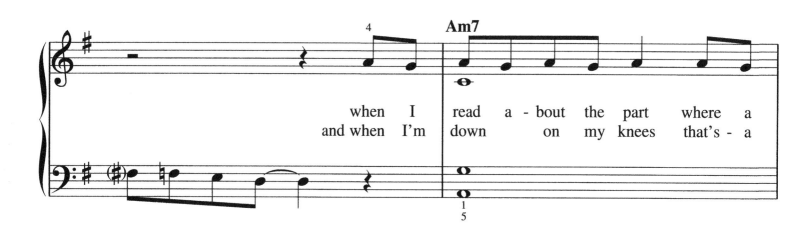

when I read a - bout the part where a
and when I'm down on my knees that's - a

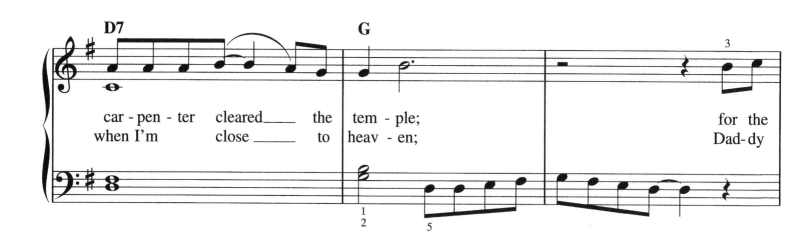

car - pen - ter cleared ___ the tem - ple;
when I'm close ___ to heav - en;

for the
Dad - dy

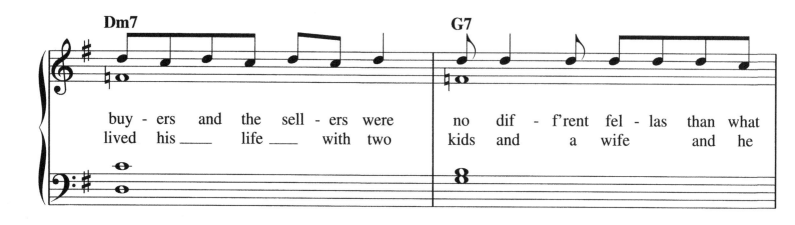

buy - ers and the sell - ers were
lived his ___ life ___ with two

no dif - f'rent fel - las than what
kids and a wife and he

115

RISE AGAIN

Words and Music by
DALLAS HOLM

Moderately, in 2

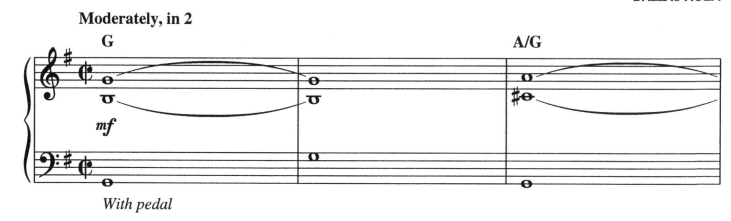

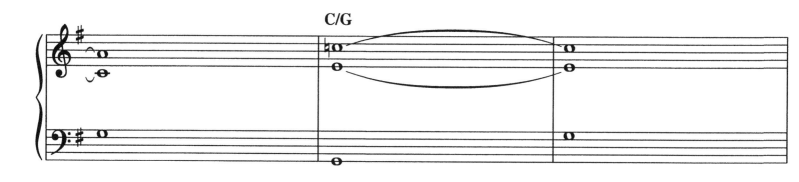

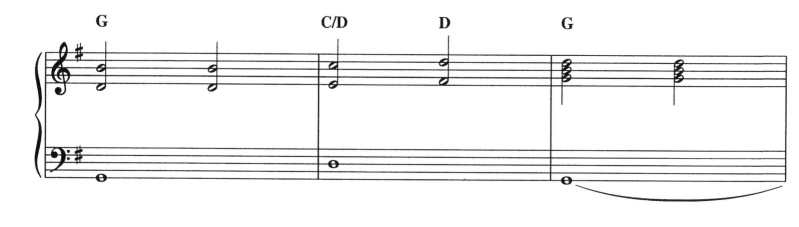

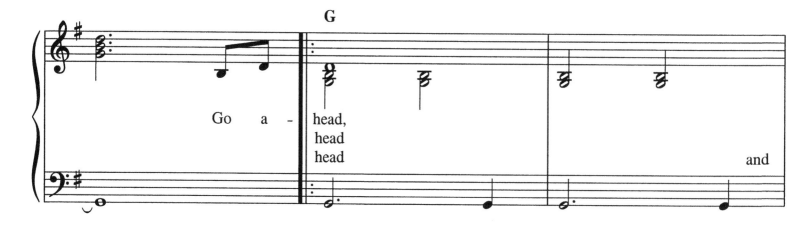

Go a- head,
head
head

and

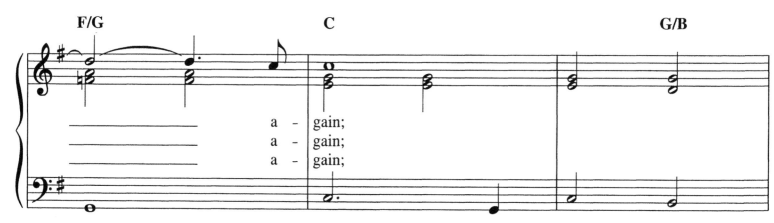

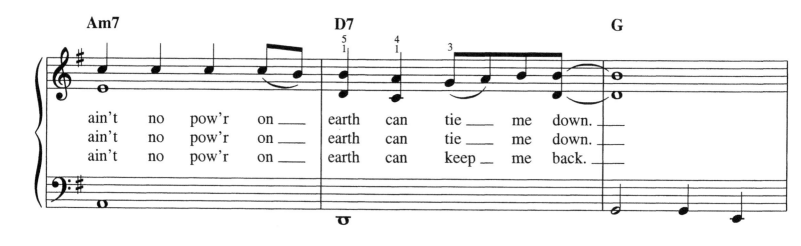

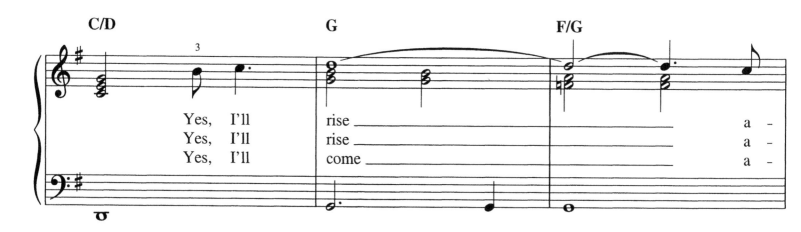

ROCK OF AGES

Words by AUGUSTUS M. TOPLADY
Altered by THOMAS COTTERILL
Music by THOMAS HASTINGS

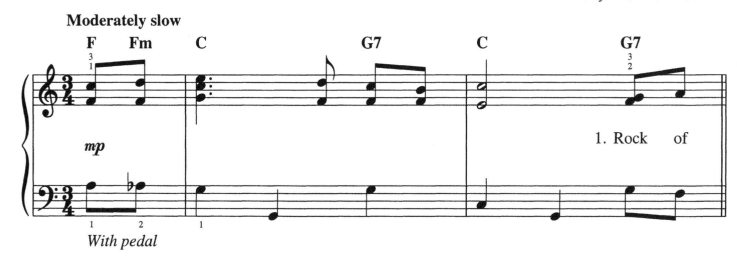

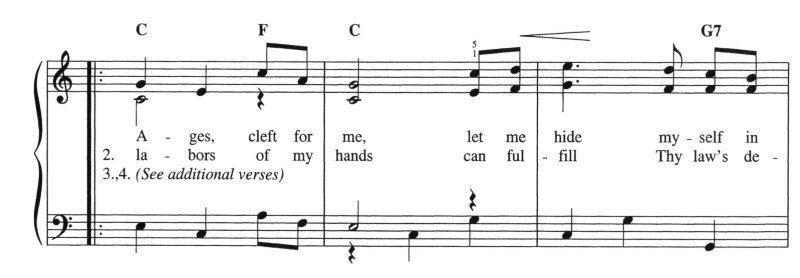

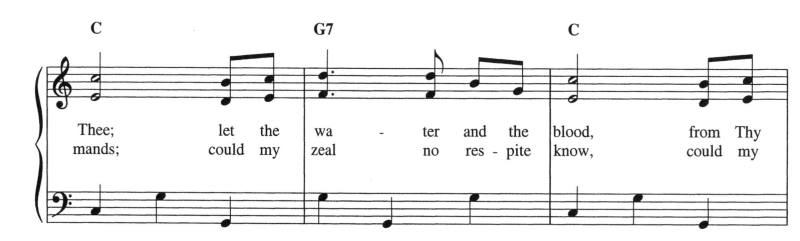

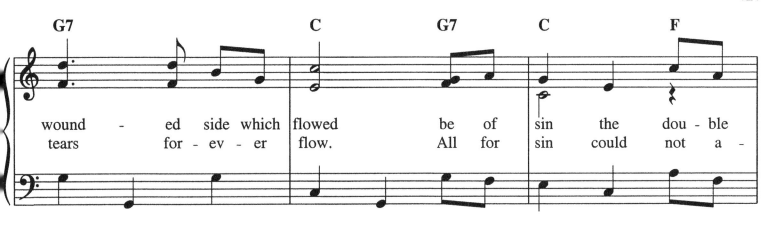

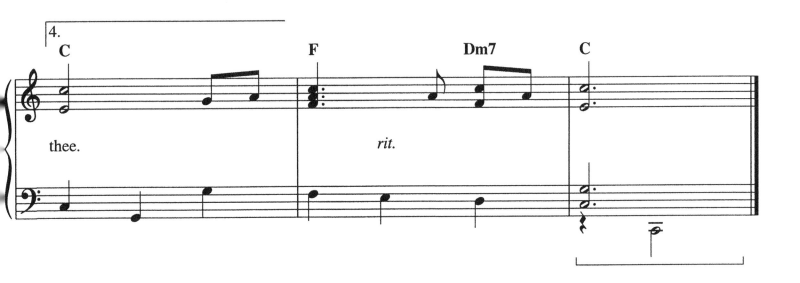

Additional Verses

3. Nothing in my hand I bring,
   Simply to the cross I cling;
   Naked, come to Thee for dress;
   Helpless, look to Thee for grace.
   Foul, I to the fountain fly;
   Wash me, Savior, or I die.

4. While I draw this fleeting breath,
   When mine eyes shall close in death.
   When I soar to worlds unknown,
   See Thee on Thy judgment throne.
   Rock of Ages, cleft for me,
   Let me hide myself in Thee.

SINCE JESUS CAME INTO MY HEART

Words by RUFUS H. McDANIEL
Music by CHARLES H. GABRIEL

Je - sus came in - to my heart, since

Je - sus came in - to my heart; floods of joy o'er my soul like the

sea bil-lows roll, since Je - sus came in - to my heart. I shall

heart, since Je - sus came in - to my heart.

THE SUN'S COMING UP

Words and Music by
DEE GASKIN

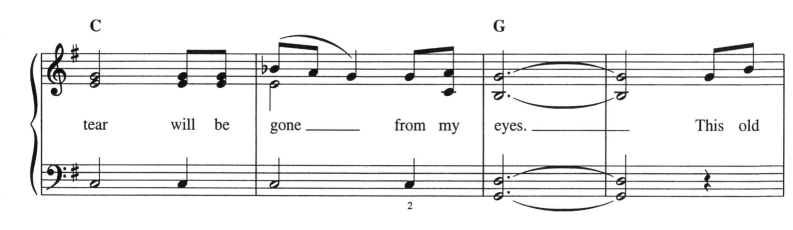

tear   will   be   gone _____ from my   eyes. _____   This old

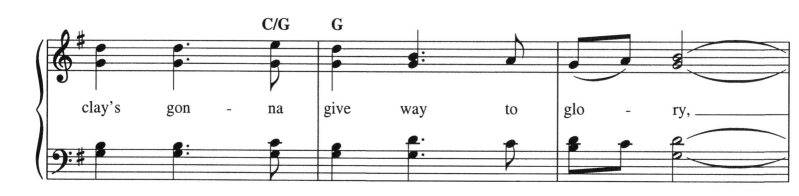

clay's   gon - na   give   way   to   glo - ry, _____

_____   and   like   an   ea - gle,   I'll   take   to   the

sky. _____   In   a   sky.

SWEET, SWEET SPIRIT

By DORIS AKERS

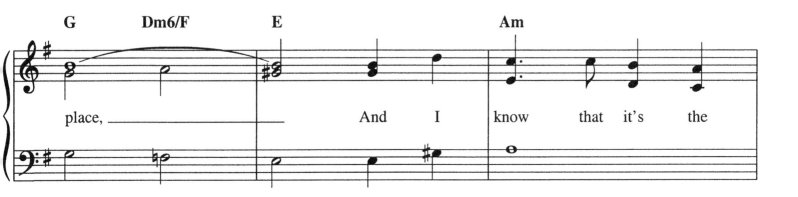

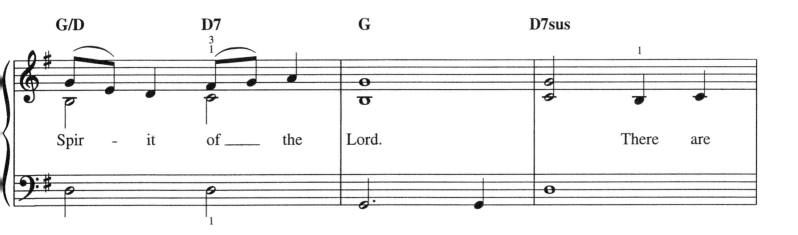

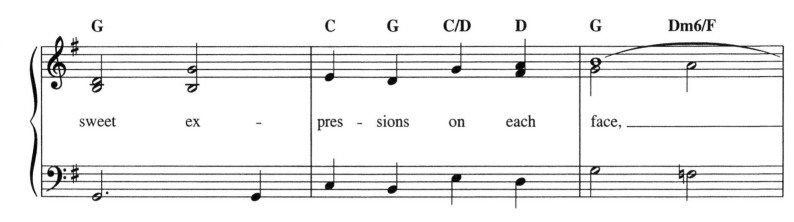

sweet ex - pres - sions on each face, _____

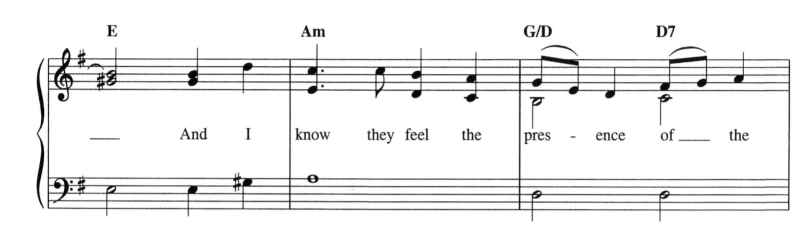

_____ And I know they feel the pres - ence of ___ the

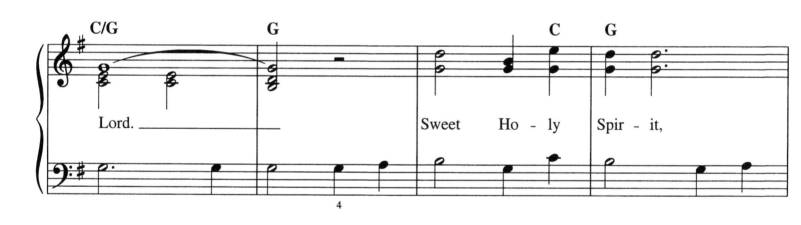

Lord. _____ Sweet Ho - ly Spir - it,

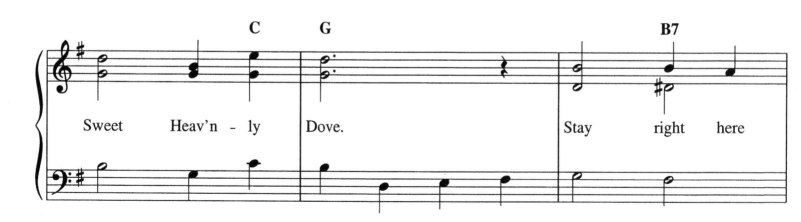

Sweet Heav'n - ly Dove. Stay right here

SWEET BY AND BY

Words by SANFORD FILLMORE BENNETT
Music by JOSEPH P. WEBSTER

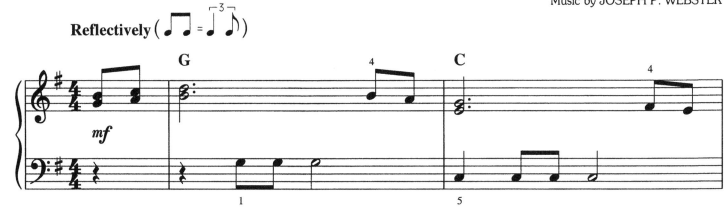

1. There's a land that is fair - er than
2. sing on that beau - ti - ful
3. (See additional lyrics)

day, and by faith we can see it a - far; for the
shore the me - lo - di - ous songs of the blest; and our

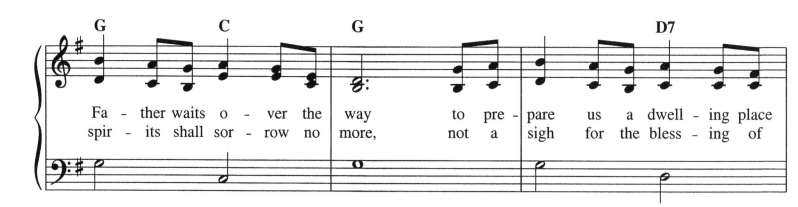

Fa - ther waits o - ver the way to pre - pare us a dwell - ing place
spir - its shall sor - row no more, not a sigh for the bless - ing of

Additional Lyrics

3. To our bountiful Father above
We will offer our tribute of praise,
For the glorious gift of His love
And the blessings that hallow our days.
Chorus

THERE'S SOMETHING ABOUT THAT NAME

Words by WILLIAM J. and GLORIA GAITHER
Music by WILLIAM J. GAITHER

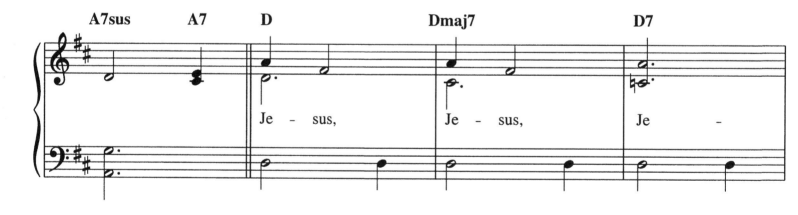

Je - sus, Je - sus, Je -

sus; There's just some - thing ___ a - bout that

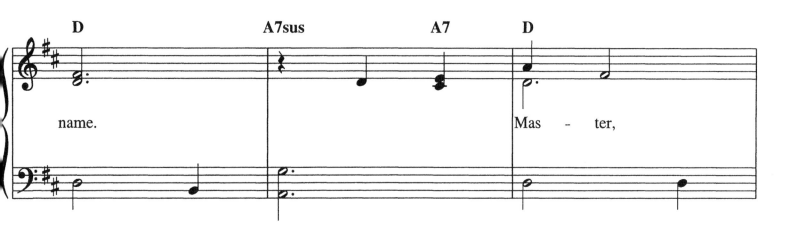

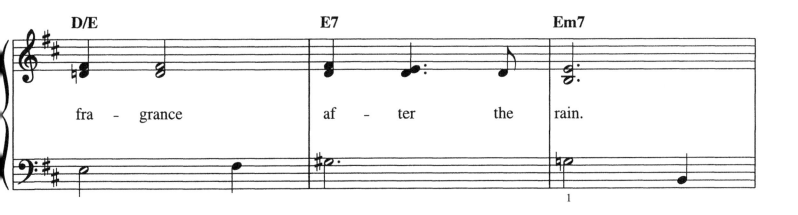

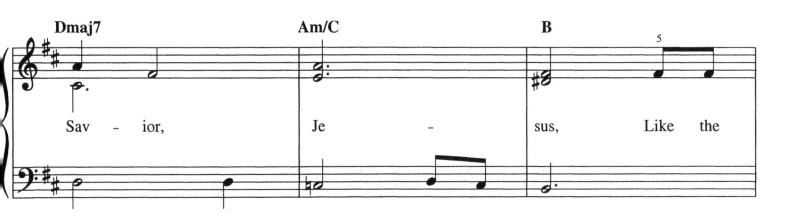

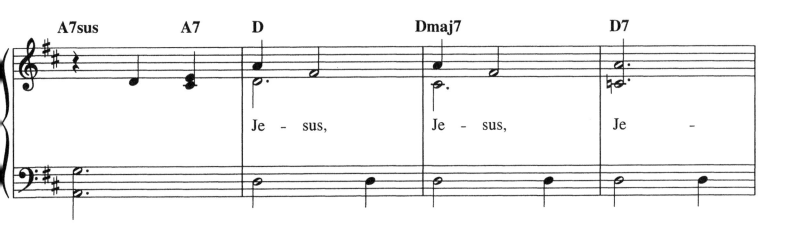

sus,　　Let all　Heav - en _____ and earth　pro -

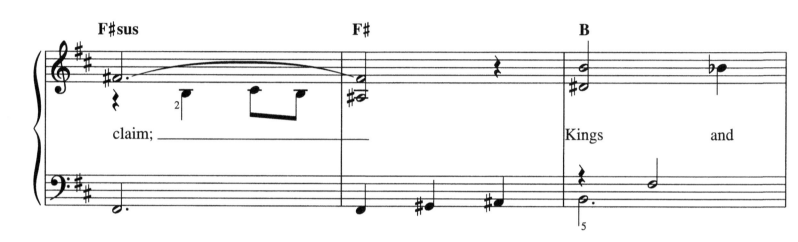

claim; _____　Kings　　and

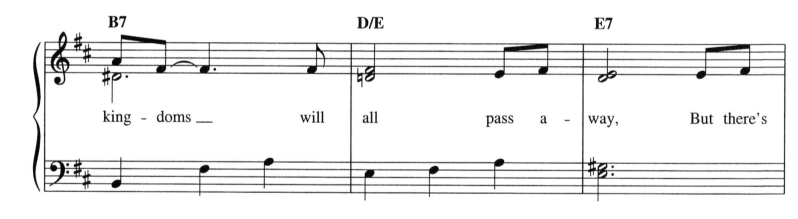

king - doms __ will all　　pass a - way,　But there's

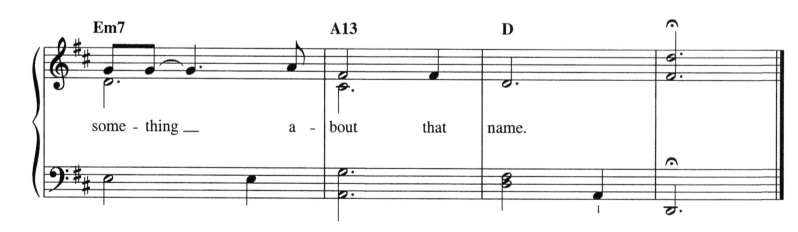

some - thing __ a - bout that name.

TURN YOUR RADIO ON

Words and Music by
ALBERT E. BRUMLEY

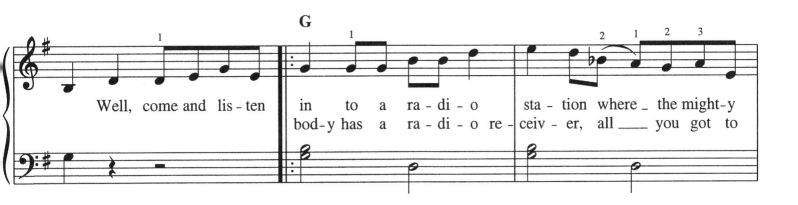

Well, come and lis-ten in to a ra-di-o sta-tion where the might-y
bod-y has a ra-di-o re-ceiv-er, all you got to

hosts of heav-en sing. Turn your ra-di-o on,
do is lis-ten for the call. Turn your ra-di-o on,

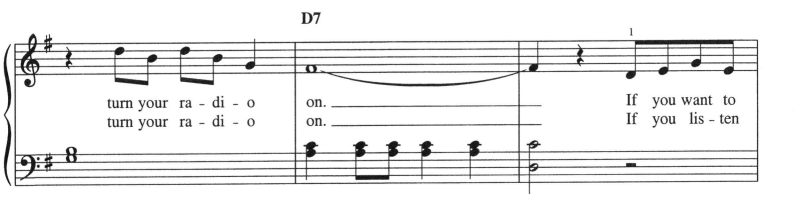

turn your ra-di-o on. If you want to
turn your ra-di-o on. If you lis-ten

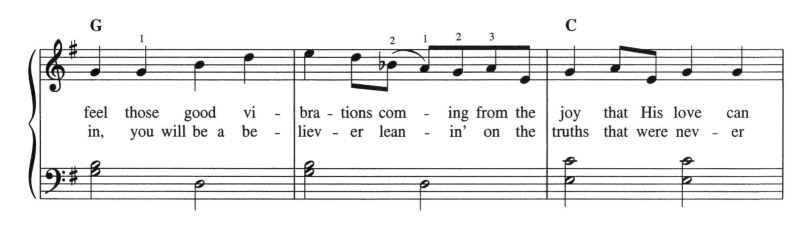

feel those good vi - bra - tions com - ing from the joy that His love can
in, you will be a be - liev - er lean - in' on the truths that were nev - er

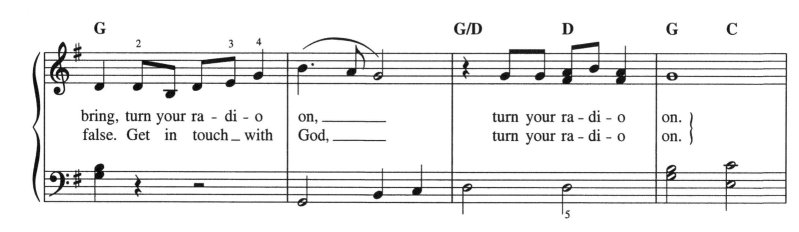

bring, turn your ra - di - o on, _____ turn your ra - di - o on.)
false. Get in touch _ with God, _____ turn your ra - di - o on. }

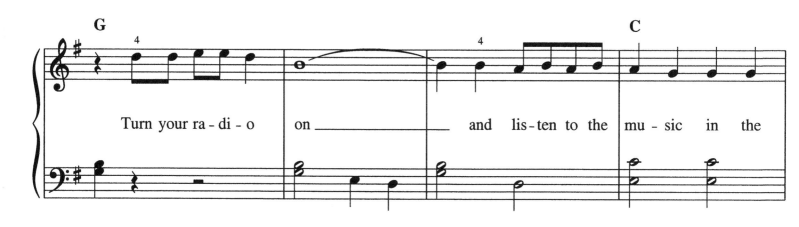

Turn your ra - di - o on _____ and lis - ten to the mu - sic in the

air. Turn your ra - di - o on, _____ heav-en's glo - ry

TURN! TURN! TURN!
(To Everything There Is a Season)

Words from the Book of Ecclesiastes
Adaptation and Music by PETE SEEGER

Moderately slow, in 2

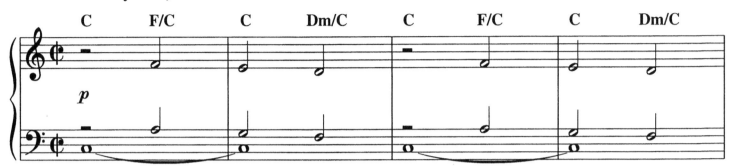

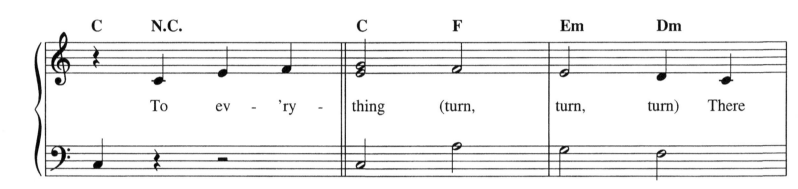

To ev - 'ry - thing (turn, turn, turn) There

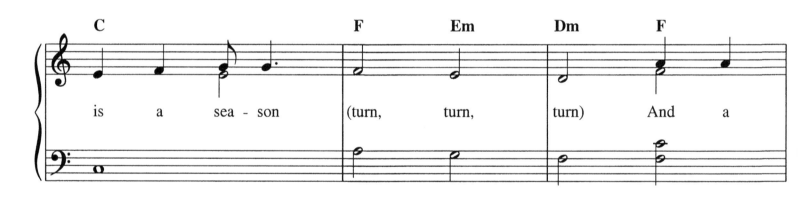

is a sea - son (turn, turn, turn) And a

time for ev - 'ry pur - pose un - der hea - ven.

139

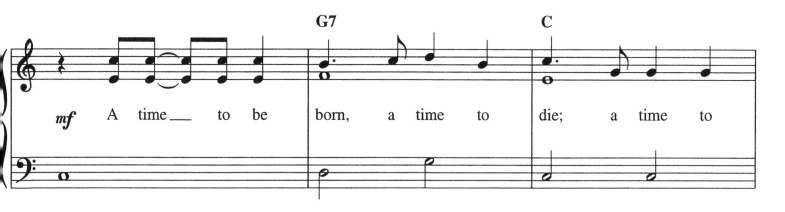

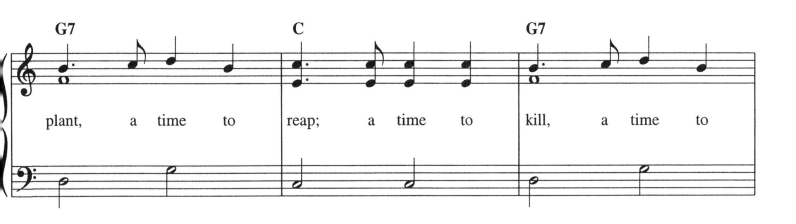

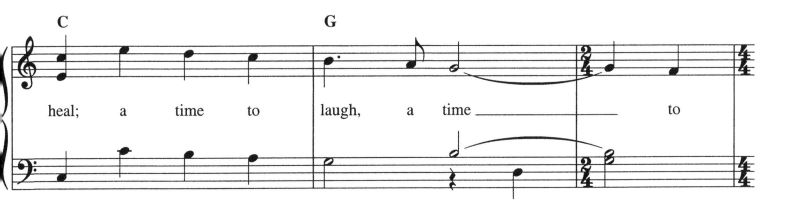

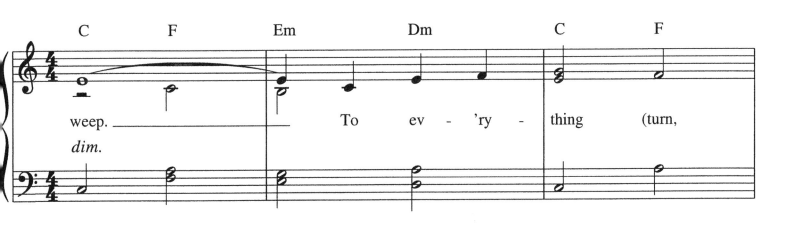

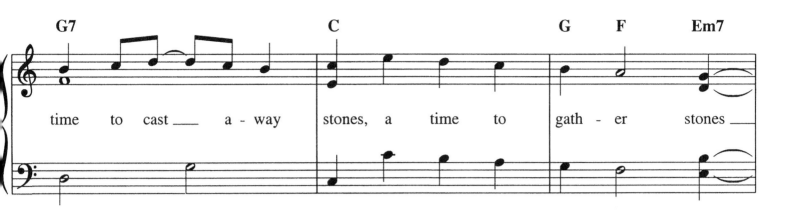

time to cast _____ a - way stones, a time to gath - er stones _____

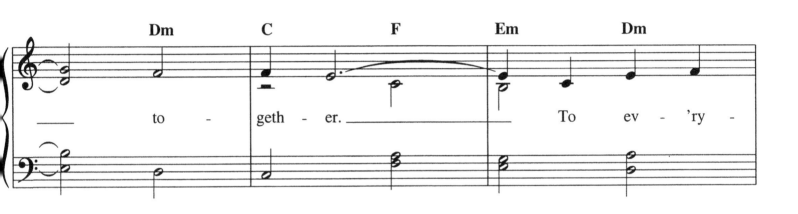

_____ to - geth - er. _____ To ev - 'ry -

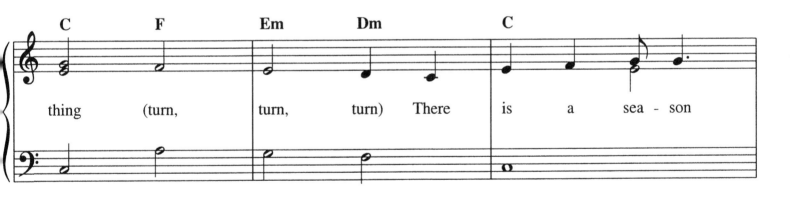

thing (turn, turn, turn) There is a sea - son

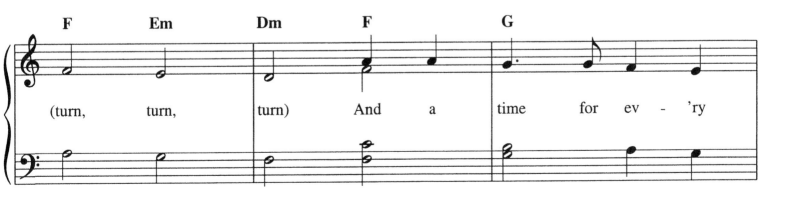

(turn, turn, turn) And a time for ev - 'ry

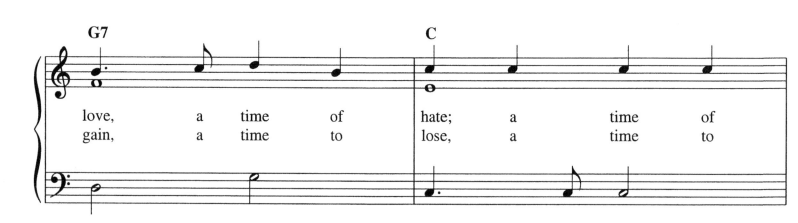

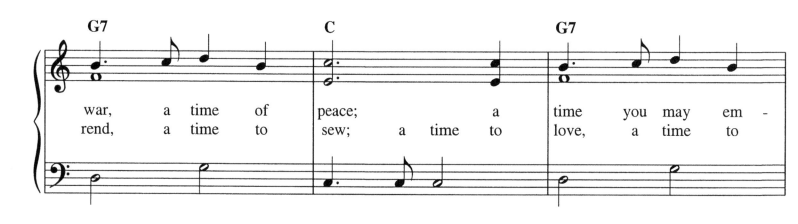

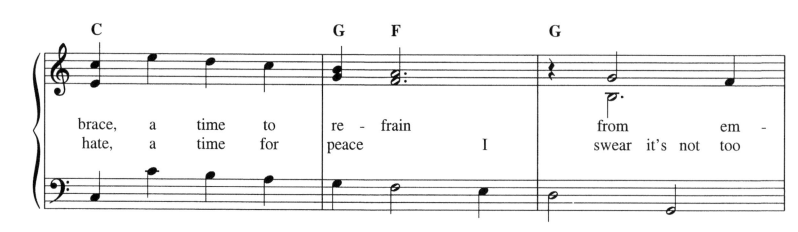

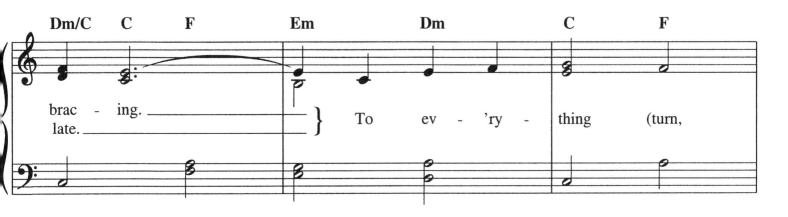

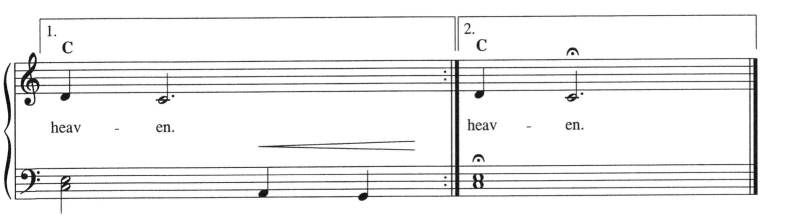

WHEN THE ROLL IS CALLED UP YONDER

Words and Music by
JAMES M. BLACK

Additional Lyrics

3. Let us labor for the Master from the dawn till setting sun,
   Let us talk of all His wondrous love and care;
   Then when all of life is over and our work on earth is done
   And the roll is called up yonder, I'll be there!
   Chorus

WHISPERING HOPE

Words and Music by
ALICE HAWTHORNE

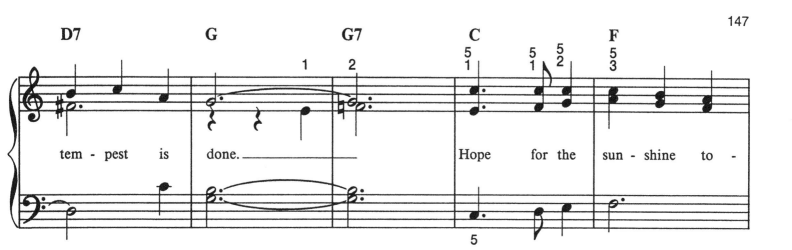

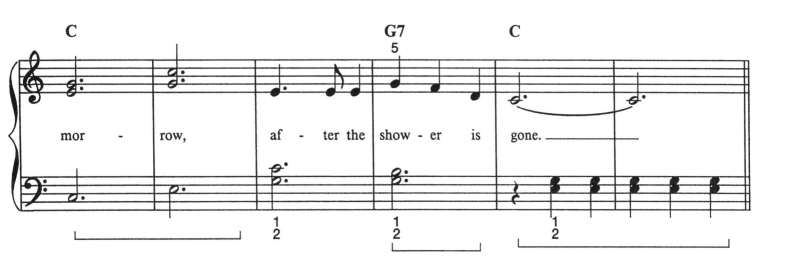

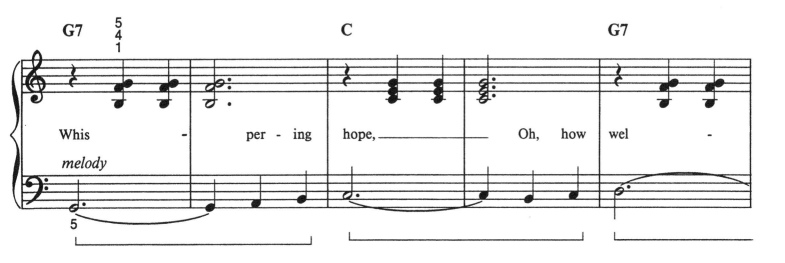

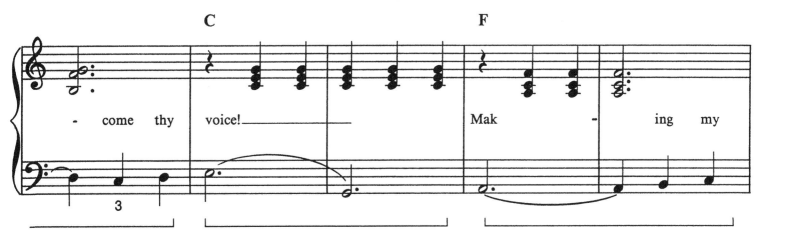

WILL THE CIRCLE BE UNBROKEN

Words by ADA R. HABERSHON
Music by CHARLES H. GABRIEL

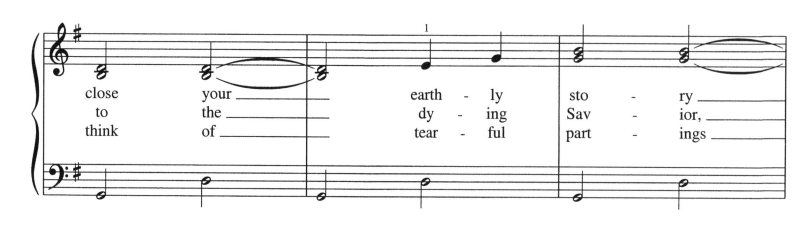

close your _____ earth - ly sto - ry _____
to the _____ dy - ing Sav - ior, _____
think of _____ tear - ful part - ings _____

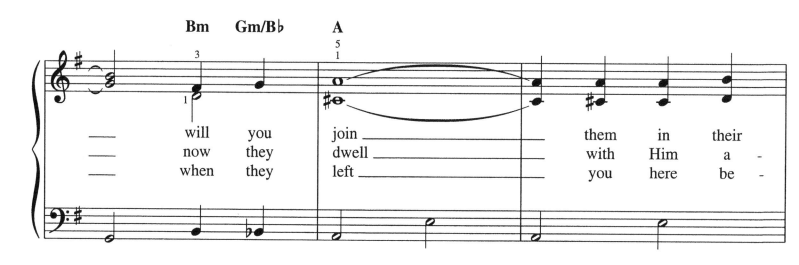

Bm   Gm/B♭   A

_____ will you join _____ them in their
_____ now they dwell _____ with Him a -
_____ when they left _____ you here be -

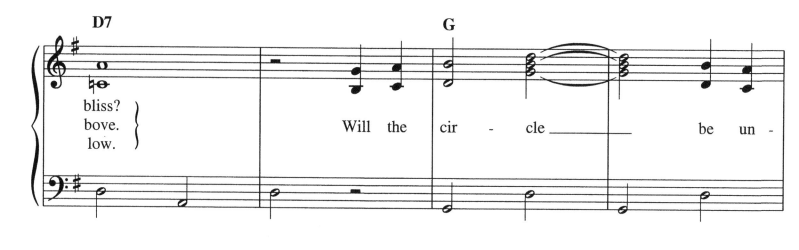

D7   G

bliss? ⎫
bove. ⎬   Will the cir - cle _____ be un -
low. ⎭

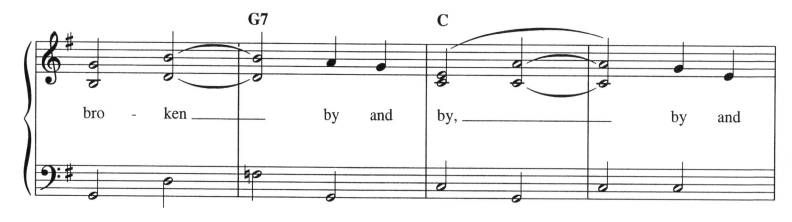

G7   C

bro - ken _____ by and by, _____ by and

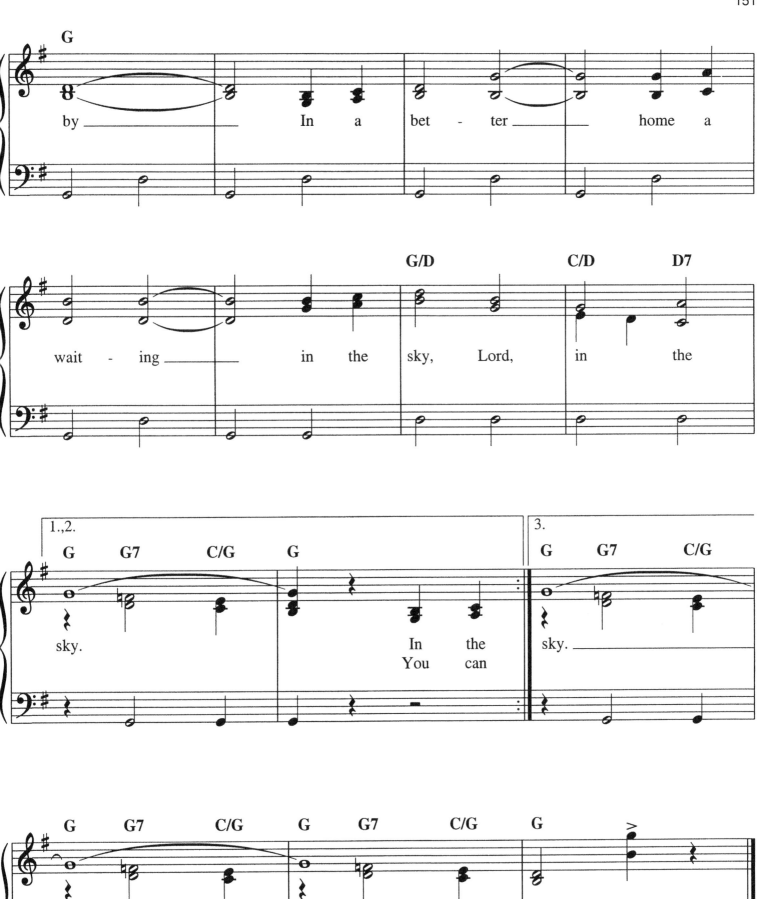

WHY ME?
(Why Me, Lord?)

Words and Music by
KRIS KRISTOFFERSON

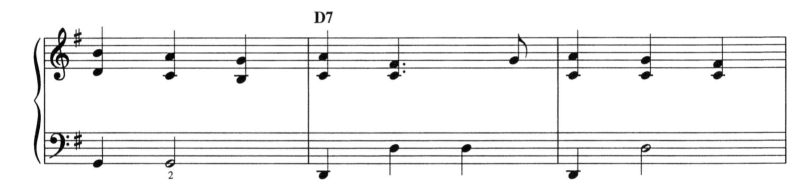

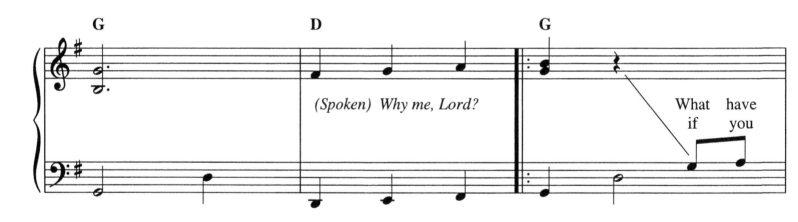

(Spoken) Why me, Lord?

What if you have

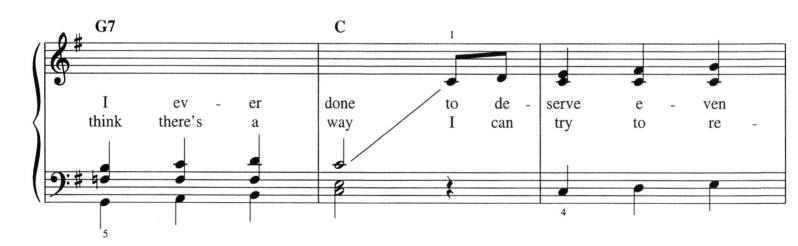

I ev- er done way I can serve e- ven
think there's a to de- try to re-

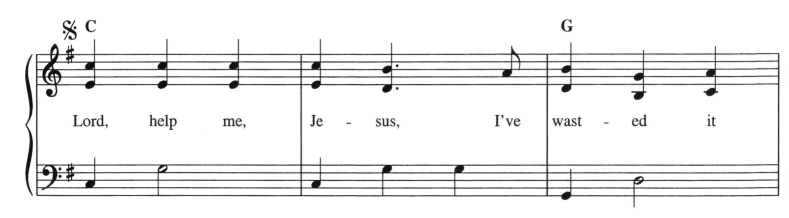

Lord, help me, Je - sus, I've wast - ed it

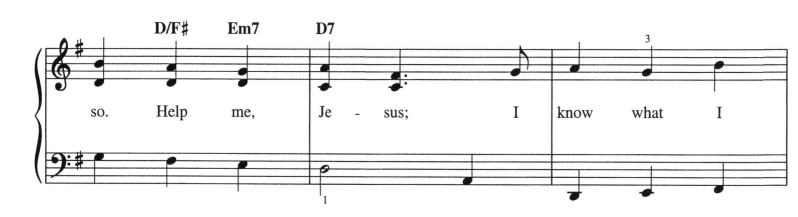

so. Help me, Je - sus; I know what I

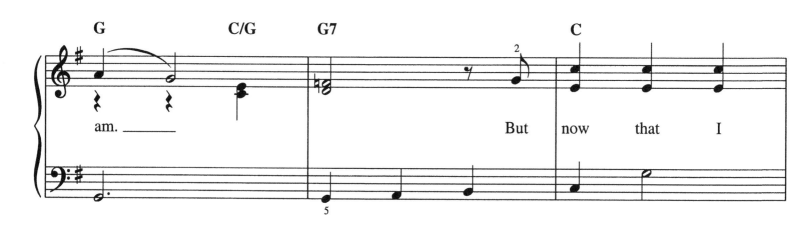

am. _____ But now that I

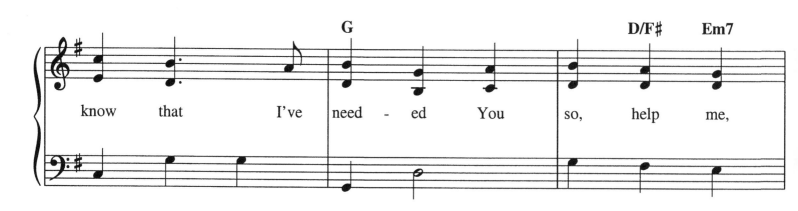

know that I've need - ed You so, help me,

WINGS OF A DOVE

Words and Music by
BOB FERGUSON

Moderate Waltz

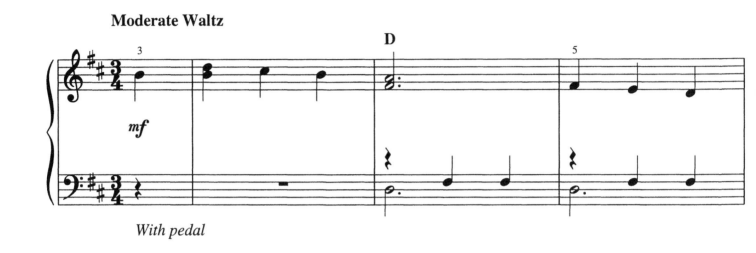

With pedal

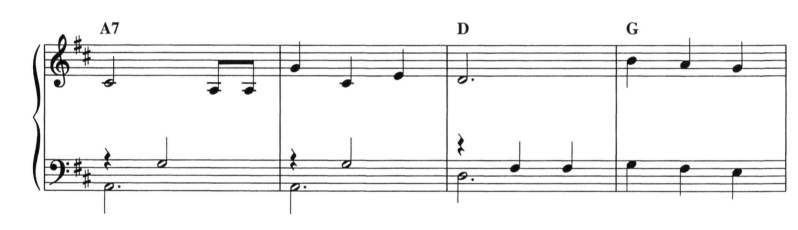

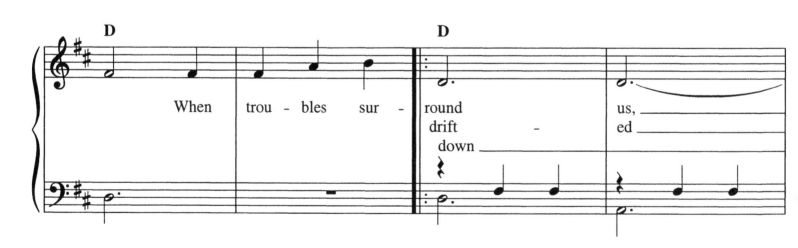

When trou - bles sur - round us,

drift - ed

down

us,

ed

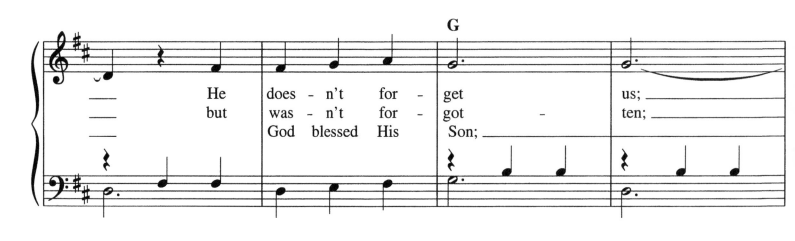

He   does – n't   for – get   us; _____
but   was – n't   for – got   –   ten; _____
God   blessed   His   Son; _____

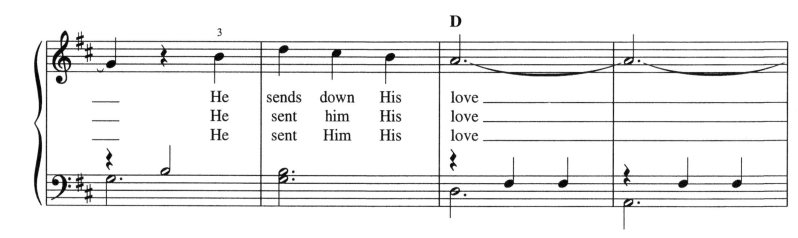

He   sends   down   His   love _____
He   sent   him   His   love _____
He   sent   Him   His   love _____

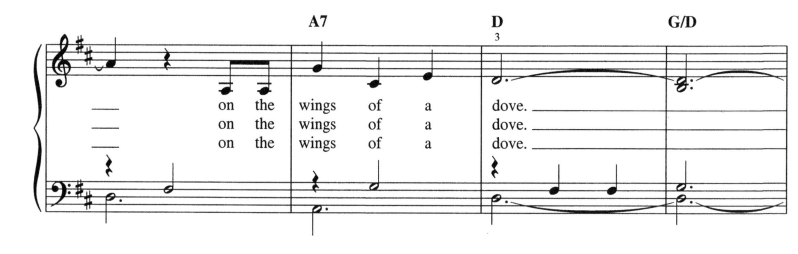

on   the   wings   of   a   dove. _____
on   the   wings   of   a   dove. _____
on   the   wings   of   a   dove. _____

On   the   wings   of   a   snow   white

The Best
PRAISE & WORSHIP
Songbooks for Piano

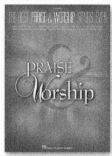

Above All
THE PHILLIP KEVEREN SERIES
15 beautiful praise song piano solo arrangements by Phillip Keveren. Includes: Above All • Agnus Dei • Breathe • Draw Me Close • He Is Exalted • I Stand in Awe • Step by Step • We Fall Down • You Are My King (Amazing Love) • and more.
00311024 Piano Solo..................................$12.99

Blended Worship Piano Collection
Songs include: Amazing Grace (My Chains Are Gone) • Be Thou My Vision • Cornerstone • Fairest Lord Jesus • Great Is Thy Faithfulness • How Great Is Our God • I Will Rise • Joyful, Joyful, We Adore Thee • Lamb of God • Majesty • Open the Eyes of My Heart • Praise to the Lord, the Almighty • Shout to the Lord • 10,000 Reasons (Bless the Lord) • Worthy Is the Lamb • Your Name • and more.
00293528 Piano Solo $17.99

Blessings
THE PHILLIP KEVEREN SERIES
Phillip Keveren delivers another stellar collection of piano solo arrangements perfect for any reverent or worship setting: Blessed Be Your Name • Blessings • Cornerstone • Holy Spirit • This Is Amazing Grace • We Believe • Your Great Name • Your Name • and more.
00156601 Piano Solo $12.99

The Best Praise & Worship Songs Ever
80 all-time favorites: Awesome God • Breathe • Days of Elijah • Here I Am to Worship • I Could Sing of Your Love Forever • Open the Eyes of My Heart • Shout to the Lord • We Bow Down • dozens more.
00311057 P/V/G..$22.99

The Big Book of Praise & Worship
Over 50 worship favorites are presented in this popular "Big Book" series collection. Includes: Always • Cornerstone • Forever Reign • I Will Follow • Jesus Paid It All • Lord, I Need You • Mighty to Save • Our God • Stronger • 10,000 Reasons (Bless the Lord) • This Is Amazing Grace • and more.
00140795 P/V/G $24.99

Contemporary Worship Duets
arr. Bill Wolaver
Contains 8 powerful songs carefully arranged by Bill Wolaver as duets for intermediate-level players: Agnus Dei • Be unto Your Name • He Is Exalted • Here I Am to Worship • I Will Rise • The Potter's Hand • Revelation Song • Your Name.
00290593 Piano Duets $10.99

The Best of Passion
Over 40 worship favorites featuring the talents of David Crowder, Matt Redman, Chris Tomlin, and others. Songs include: Always • Awakening • Blessed Be Your Name • Jesus Paid It All • My Heart Is Yours • Our God • 10,000 Reasons (Bless the Lord) • and more.
00101888 P/V/G $19.99

Praise & Worship Duets
THE PHILLIP KEVEREN SERIES
8 worshipful duets by Phillip Keveren: As the Deer • Awesome God • Give Thanks • Great Is the Lord • Lord, I Lift Your Name on High • Shout to the Lord • There Is a Redeemer • We Fall Down.
00311203 Piano Duet................................$12.99

Shout to the Lord!
THE PHILLIP KEVEREN SERIES
14 favorite praise songs, including: As the Deer • El Shaddai • Give Thanks • Great Is the Lord • How Beautiful • More Precious Than Silver • Oh Lord, You're Beautiful • A Shield About Me • Shine, Jesus, Shine • Shout to the Lord • Thy Word • and more.
00310699 Piano Solo $14.99

Sunday Solos in the Key of C
CLASSIC & CONTEMPORARY WORSHIP SONGS
22 C-major selections, including: Above All • Good Good Father • His Name Is Wonderful • Holy Spirit • Lord, I Need You • Reckless Love • What a Beautiful Name • You Are My All in All • and more.
00301044 Piano Solo $14.99

The Chris Tomlin Collection – 2nd Edition
15 songs from one of the leading artists and composers in Contemporary Christian music, including the favorites: Amazing Grace (My Chains Are Gone) • Holy Is the Lord • How Can I Keep from Singing • How Great Is Our God • Jesus Messiah • Our God • We Fall Down • and more.
00306951 P/V/G $17.99

Top Christian Downloads
21 of Christian music's top hits are presented in this collection of intermediate level piano solo arrangements. Includes: Forever Reign • How Great Is Our God • Mighty to Save • Praise You in This Storm • 10,000 Reasons (Bless the Lord) • Your Grace Is Enough • and more.
00125051 Piano Solo..................................$14.99

Top 25 Worship Songs
25 contemporary worship hits includes: Glorious Day (Passion) • Good, Good Father (Chris Tomlin) • Holy Spirit (Francesca Battistelli) • King of My Heart (John Mark & Sarah McMillan) • The Lion and the Lamb (Big Daddy Weave) • Reckless Love (Cory Asbury) • 10,000 Reasons (Matt Redman) • This Is Amazing Grace (Phil Wickham) • What a Beautiful Name (Hillsong Worship) • and more.
00288610 P/V/G $17.99

Top Worship Downloads
20 of today's chart-topping Christian hits, including: Cornerstone • Forever Reign • Great I Am • Here for You • Lord, I Need You • My God • Never Once • One Thing Remains (Your Love Never Fails) • Your Great Name • and more.
00120870 P/V/G $16.99

The World's Greatest Praise Songs
Shawnee Press
This is a unique and useful collection of 50 of the very best praise titles of the last three decades. Includes: Above All • Forever • Here I Am to Worship • I Could Sing of Your Love Forever • Open the Eyes of My Heart • and so many more.
35022891 P/V/G $19.99